Jesus

The Compassion of God

THEOLOGY AND LIFE SERIES

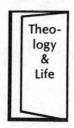

Volume 9

Jesus

The Compassion of God

New Perspectives

on the

Tradition of Christianity

by

Monika K. Hellwig

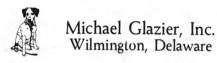

Michael Glazier, Inc.
Wilmington, Delaware

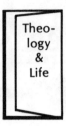

Theo-
logy
&
Life

ABOUT THE AUTHOR

Monika K. Hellwig is Professor of Theology at Georgetown University. Among her many publications are *The Eucharist and The Hunger of the World*; *Understanding Catholicism*; and *Sign of Reconciliation and Conversion: The Sacrament of Penance for Our Times*, which is published in The Message of the Sacraments series of which she is the Editor.

First published in 1983 by Michael Glazier Inc., 1723 Delaware Avenue, Wilmington, Delaware 19806 ● Distributed outside the U.S., Canada and Philippines by Dominican Publications, St. Saviour's, Dublin 1, Ireland ● ©1983 by Monika K. Hellwig. All rights reserved. ●Library of Congress Card Catalog Number: 83-81998 ● International Standard Book Numbers: Theology and Life Series, 0-89453-295-2; Jesus 0-89453-365-7 (Michael Glazier, Inc.); 0-907271-26-X (Dominican Publications) ● Cover design by Lillian Brulc ● Printed in the United States of America

To Piet Schoonenberg, S.J.

    a courageous and visionary scholar
    an artist in encouragement
    an inspiration to many
    and a wonderful friend

this book is gratefully dedicated

CONTENTS

Acknowledgements

This book owes its existence in large measure to the kindness of my departmental chairman, William McFadden, S.J., my other colleagues in the Theology Department, and the Provost and Academic Vice-President of Georgetown University, Donald J. Freeze, S.J., who made a summer research fellowship and a sabbatical available to me. The book is also the response to the kindly interest and encouragement of Michael Glazier and Eileen Carzo of Michael Glazier, Inc.

Beyond the published sources to which my indebtedness is acknowledged in footnotes and bibliography, there are many scholars whose living presence has influenced my thought in Christology, notably my colleagues in several projects of the Woodstock Theological Center. Moreover, without the scholarly expertise and unfailing courteous, friendly help of the Woodstock librarians, it would have taken me several more years to prepare to write this book than it did, in fact, take. I am, however, most particularly indebted to Gerard Sloyan, and most of all to Piet Schoonenberg, S.J., to whom this volume is dedicated.

Georgetown University
July 22nd, Feast of St. Mary Magdalene, 1983

Introduction: The Present State of the Question in the Theoretical Structure of Christology

Contemporary Christians find themselves burdened and obstructed in their faith by the conventional theoretical structure of Christology. This becomes increasingly clear. It is not that they think the claims made for the person of Jesus are too great, but rather that these claims are not intelligible. It has, of course, always been claimed that we are approaching a mystery of revelation which reason can not encompass. Yet the conventional structure of Christology is a rational discourse which implicitly but quite clearly claims intelligibility.

This problem in itself is not new at all. Paul of Tarsus, Justin the Martyr, Origen, the Antiochenes and Alexandrians, the Fathers of Chalcedon, as well as Hilary, Ambrose and Augustine in the West, and Anselm, Thomas Aquinas, Duns Scotus and others among the mediaeval scholastics, were all aware of the tension involved in the doing of Christian theology in general and in the construction of a Christology in particular. But in every age and culture the tension and the problem have been shaped in characteristic and particular ways. In times of growth and vigor the answers have also been sought in characteristic and particular ways. Only in times of decadence and decline have the answers from another time and an alien culture been accepted as finished, sufficient and in a form that must remain forever.

In our own times many cultural developments converge to make the established explanations in Christology less and less helpful. The question of truth in religious assertions is, of course, not a simple or self-evident matter. We are making assertions that reach beyond experience and therefore are not concerned with "facts" in the ordinary sense of that word. There are basically two models by which one might understand what is happening in religious and theological discourse. One of these is a process of speculation by inference from what we know and experience to the realms of reality supposed to lie beyond our experience. The other is a process of interpretation, or thematization, of experience itself in its more elusive dimensions.

If theology is understood as a speculative process, then it begins with what are understood to be facts. It searches for a coherent explanation of these "facts," perhaps in terms of causality, or perhaps in terms of finality, or in very broad categories of significance or intelligibility. The process is understood as strictly rational, a matter of applying the rules of logical thinking in order to conjecture correctly from the known to the unknown and to arrive at the correct answer which is given in the reality that lies beyond thought, precedes thought, and is the object of thought. The answer obtained in such a process is either right or wrong. A complex conclusion may be partly right and partly wrong, but when it is broken down into its component parts each of these is either right or wrong.

This, of course, describes an ideal type, seldom if ever found in its pure form. However, it will be apparent that to the extent that this is seen as the proper model in theology, to that extent the formulations will be seen as unchangeable when they have been given formal hierarchic endorsement or have become standard teaching. To change such formulations would be to admit that the tradition is in error and does not offer a reliable foundation for the faith. In the realm of Christology this would be particularly sensitive.

Applying this model in its crudest form in Christology, one might arrive at some such basic framework as the following. The "facts" of the Gospels and letters of the New Testament are the following: Jesus claimed to be divine, worked miracles, prophesied events which actually came to pass, and rose from the dead. The inference to be drawn from this combination is that his claims must be true, and therefore he must be divine. Further "facts" are: he was truly born, he ate and drank, walked and talked and worked, and he suffered and truly died. The inference is that he must be human. Therefore we have a man who is also divine. But to be divine ("fact" understood to be "known" from philosophy) means to be eternal, without beginning or end, without before or after. It means to possess all knowledge simultaneously and to be all-powerful (also "self-evident" or at least inferable "facts" known from reason). Therefore, as divine, Jesus is eternally pre-existent though as human he has a beginning in time. As divine he is all-knowing and all-powerful though as human he is limited in knowledge and in power.

Further inferences drawn from this must then accommodate the "known" properties of the divine with the known properties of the human in the one person, Jesus. Inevitably this involves certain compromises in the description of his human experience, making his inner life rather remote from anything that we would recognize from our own experience of being human. However, the logic of the argument demands these compromises at each stage and they must therefore be true. If they are true at any time, they are always true and will always continue to be true in the future, because the facts have been established in the past and therefore cannot change. There is, of course, the theoretical possibility that new facts should come to light or that old facts should be revealed in a different perspective. However, when conclusions have been authoritatively endorsed or even when they have become standard teaching, there must needs be massive resistance against this possibility, because this model of theology is understood to allow only right or wrong answers, and if new facts come to light and change the conclusions then what was taught in the past was simply wrong.

If this ideal type were followed consistently, it would be reasonable to expect massive resistance to change. It would be axiomatic that truth is truth and does not change "with every whim and fancy." We claim to deal with truth about the eternal, and that means we deal with eternal truth. There cannot, therefore, be change in it, though there might perchance be change in our knowledge or understanding of it. Such change could only be a further penetration into the understanding of the truth or a discovery that what we thought we knew was based on misinformation or misunderstanding. Contemporary Christology, when implicitly using this model more than the other, has in fact been confronted with both kinds of change quite extensively. For instance, more information about the New Testament use of such words as *kyrios* has provided a basis for further penetration into the understanding of the divinity claim. More information about the literary genres of the New Testament has corrected the foundations on which much Christological reasoning was based.

In both these types of new factual information scholars have found an imperative to rethink and reformulate some Christological arguments. In itself this is not a problem even within a purely rational model of theology. Theoretically this was always foreseen by those who operated within the model. The problem arises when the pursuit of the argument leads to conclusions that cannot be reduced to the classic, authoritative formulations, such as those of Chalcedon. If those classic formulations simply present the changeless truth, then all further discussion, no matter how subtle, no matter how newly well-informed, must still be reducible to those formulations.

It is, of course, possible that the new discussions should deal with new matter that was not a subject of the classic formulations, such as the relationship of the Incarnation and Resurrection to the practical possibility of permanent peace in the world. In this case there may be a certain incongruence between the traditional formulation and the new discussion and conclusion, but there will nevertheless be no direct conflict. If, however, the new discussions deal with such matter as the old formulations have claimed to cover comprehensively, there may be a direct contradiction. Such is the case, for instance, when there is discussion of what it means to be human and the role that personhood has in being and becoming human, more particularly when such discussion comes to the conclusion that to be truly human can only mean to be a human person. Such discussion then draws a conclusion that contradicts the formulation that has become standard teaching.

On the rational model of theology this contradiction is intolerable. One of the conclusions is right and the other must be wrong. What was right before continues to be right, so there must be something faulty in the reasoning that led to the new position. It need not be taken seriously and had best be silenced. But this raises the question for theology in general whether historical and linguistic research, return to the sources, and approaches from varied philosophical and cultural bases, are legitimate theological enterprises at all, or whether the task of theological scholarship must always be to reason backwards from dogmatically defined or standard teachings in order to provide the justification for them. In other words the question is whether theology is a strictly finite process in which topics and questions are constantly being finished off with permanent answers which do not require further reflection and formulation.

As was mentioned before, this is an ideal type not found in its pure form. All scholars admit the analogical nature of religious language, therefore all admit that the choice of terms is in itself often arbitrary though it may become normative and mandatory by official adoption in church documents. Yet, while the model of theology as a purely rational quest to infer truth that is beyond experience, is not found in its pure form, it seems often enough to be the dominant model. Many Christians find that with this model dominant, Christology seems further and further away from the quest for a meaningful and responsible life and the quest for communion with God in their own lives.

A quite different model of theology is that of a process of interpretation or thematization of religious experience. In this understanding of the nature of the theological endeavor, the task is more an art than a science. Certainly it nowise claims to be an exact science. The task is to formulate an account of events and experiences and persons in images and analogies that will somehow embody or express what is in itself ineffable. One who sees the task this way is always aware of the arbitrary nature of the expressions. Paradoxes are at home here. A great variety of formulations is expected and welcomed. Truth is understood in a rather broader sense as inclusive rather than exclusive. Truth is recognized not only by a coherence that accounts for all the facts of experience, but by other types of harmony — the harmony of beauty, of consolation, of purpose in life, of challenge. The truth of a statement is known in a certain luminosity or transparence in which personal quest and tradition are both recognized as fulfilled.

It is clear that this is what happens in John's Gospel when Jesus is presented as God's Word to us, spoken into the world from the beginning, the Word that is God himself speaking. All the imagery and associations that are invoked by this do indeed converge to explain our relationship to Jesus in a way that is both consolation and challenge, both question and answer. A similar expression is that which names Jesus the light of the world, shining into the darkness. Although it is possible to elaborate each of these images quite extensively into an inclusive worldview and interpretation both of individual human destiny and of history, it is evident that the truth and viability of one does not imply the falsehood of the other. They appear rather as complementary and as adding, so to speak, to each other's truth.

What actually happens in history, of course, is that some of these expressions become normative in the language and thought of the community. So much repetition, elaboration and authority begins to build up around these normative expressions that they are perceived as quite different from other formulations in their access to and rendering of the truth. They no longer appear analogous but immediately appropriate to that of which they speak. Theology as rational argumentation begins to be based on these expressions. Then, because rational argumentation culminates in a conclusion which, it is understood, must be either right or wrong, there is a retrospective effect canonizing a poetic image or analogy that may have been only one side of a paradox when first formulated.

There is, of course, the problem in such a canonizing of imagery that as culture and language change, the old images and analogies carry less and less effective meaning to succeeding generations. Yet this is a lesser problem and even an inevitable one, for any tradition must necessarily keep building bridges of empathy and imagination that will bring its followers to the classic symbols on which the tradition is founded. The more serious problem is the danger that theological thought may become quite sterile spiritually and quite incompetent to deal with the practical (particularly the public) dimensions of contemporary life. That danger arises from the fact that the process as described above has a tendency to foreclose discussion on questions that do not fit into the established paradigms. In our times this particular danger looms large.

A perennial temptation, then, to which theologians seem all too ready to yield, is that of paying lip-service to that transcendence of the mysteries of faith which renders them essentially incomprehensible, inexhaustible and ineffable, but then immediately proceeding to discuss these same mysteries by methods incompatible with that acknowledgement. Nowhere is this more clearly the case than in the discussion concerning the "person" and "natures" of Jesus, interlocked with the discussion of the "nature" and "persons" of the triune God. Not least of the difficulties here is the often unperceived semantic shift within the discussion, for the word "person" is not used univocally when discussing the "three persons" in the triune God and the "one person" of Jesus.

It seems, therefore, unfortunate that Christology should be permanently trapped in the riddle of the "one person, two natures," which cannot be unravelled and does not lend itself to the resolving of some very urgent contemporary questions concerning the meaning of Jesus for human life, hope and relationships. There have been many attempts made to re-examine and re-interpret this traditional paradigm of Christology, some of which throw much new light on the discussions leading up to Chalcedon, the issues under debate at Chalcedon, and the subsequent developments of the elaborate traditional Christology.[1] These attempts have already been

---

[1] The primary texts, with explanatory introduction, have been collected recently by Richard A. Norris in *The Christological Controversy* (Philadelphia: Fortress, 1980). An elaborate study of the arguments is contained in *Christ in Christian Tradition*, by Aloys Grillmeier, (N.Y.: Sheed & Ward, 1964). A systematic Christology which considers the implications of the arguments and solutions for our own times is that of Pannenberg, *Jesus, God and Man* (Philadelphia: Westminster, 1968).

summarized in several published works quite recently.[2] That task will not be repeated here.

The intent of the present volume is to reflect on the Christian claims for Jesus by the method of interpreting and thematizing the Christian experience of salvation and hope arising from the impact of Jesus within the community of faith and in the world and its history at large. Such a method does not by-pass the classic images, analogies, dogmatic formulations, but it does rely upon a much wider range of sources including the neglected or discontinued images of the New Testament and the Church Fathers, and including also the later traditions of spirituality with their devotional language and lore which became in the course of time quite sharply separated from the official Christology of the dogmatic theology tradition.

More specifically , the intent of this volume is to approach the question of the meaning of Jesus from the questions raised by the various liberation movements of our times and particularly from the questions raised by Liberation Theology. This demands that Christology be approached through soteriology, that is, through reflection on the experience of the need of salvation and on the fragmentary experiences of being caught up into the process of salvation. It also demands a quest through the classic symbols and analogies, including the forgotten ones, for those representations that make luminous sense to the contemporary believer by making explicit the harmony, the purpose and the meaning of human life.

[2]*E.g.* in Jon Sobrino's *Christology at the Crossroads* (Maryknoll, N.Y.: Orbis, 1976); earlier, Norman Pittenger's *Christology Reconsidered* (London: SCM Press, 1970); and more recently, Michael L. Cook's *The Jesus of Faith* (N.Y.: Paulist, 1981). A new and very promising solution is offered by Frans Jozef van Beecke, *Christ Proclaimed: Christology as Rhetoric* (N.Y .: Paulist, 1979).

Part I

The Task of Christology

1

Christian Questions about Jesus

The first and all-inclusive question that Christians must ask and answer about Jesus is: what difference does Jesus make? It is the soteriological question that contains Christology. It is not a Christology consisting primarily of the divinity claim and its justification, which also includes a soteriology. The Christian gospel is a message about salvation from sin. It implies a dynamic, not simply an explanation of why things are the way they are. Moreover, it implies a human dynamic, played out within human freedom and therefore accessible to human experience.[1] The Christian gospel, then, demands an

---

[1]Both Henri de Lubac, in *Le surnaturel*, (Paris: Aubier, 1946) reformulated in *The Mystery of the Supernatural* (N.Y. Herder, 1967) and Karl Rahner, in his whole work but particularly in "Nature and Grace," *Theological Investigations, Vol. IV.* (Baltimore: Helicon, 1966) have solidly demonstrated that grace, the supernatural, the process of redemption must be accessible to experience.

explanation that arises from the participants' experience and finds its intelligibility with reference to that experience.

The struggle of Christian theology in our times is to re-establish effective contact with the experience of contemporary Christians. The history of the discussions of grace and of the atonement shows a process of alienation of the notion of salvation from actual Christian experience, and its transfer into categories of "hearsay" evidence that seemed to become more remote with the passage of time.[2] The new life of the resurrection which constituted the good news of the apostolic community in the New Testament, is quite obviously a matter of immediate experience giving promise of further future fulfillment. Early patristic texts continue to be based on that understanding. Even in the fourth and fifth centuries the catecheses directed to adult converts to the community by Cyril of Jerusalem, Ambrose of Milan and Augustine of Hippo are based on the assumption that these converts will know by experience in their own lives and in the life of the community the difference that Jesus makes. Something is expected to be happening that is self-validating in the human quest of these proselytes, so that they will recognize it as the grace of God which is incipient salvation.

For reasons that have been analyzed often enough elsewhere,[3] respectability, legal establishment and mass conversions without proper preparation, all worked together to change this pattern. Seldom in the mediaeval literature does

---

[2]*Cf.* H. Rondet, *Gratia Christi* (Paris: Beauchesne, 1948); and Edmund Fortman, ed., *The Theology of Man and Grace* (Milwaukee: Bruce, 1966).

[3]*E.g.* in the works of Josef Jungmann on liturgical and catechetical developments, and in those of Hans Küng on ecclesiology.

one have the sense that grace and redemption have to do with a reality known from living experience. They seem much rather to refer to a reality that is inaccessible to experience but understood to be known with certainty from the teaching of the Church. Only after death or in very exceptional mystical experiences of a favored few can salvation be expected to become part of experience.

Luther's position was, of course, in part a protest against the anxiety about one's future destiny, and against the servility towards the official guardians of the sacramental system and authority of the Church, that this understanding tended to produce. The enthusiastic sects were a protest against the disinterest and infidelity it tended to foster. Catholic theology resisted the identification of grace and salvation with emotional excitement, but in doing so seemed to reinforce the understanding that the whole process of redemption is inaccessible to human experience except beyond death. Side by side with this, however, there were strands of moral theology and spiritual theology which subtly implied the contrary. Moral theology with its rules for identifying mortal and venial sins, implied that while grace in itself was inaccessible to experience, the state of grace could be inferred from an introspective analysis of behavior. Spiritual theology, with its favorite construction of the three ways, stages or ages of the interior life, likewise implied that an analysis of behavior and attitudes and experiences in prayer, testifies to the process of redemption in the individual.

It is perhaps this last, combined with the demands of the contemporary world, that led twentieth century theologians to look at salvation in categories of present experience. It seems to be no chance connection that the two Catholic authors whose work pioneered in this, Karl Rahner[4] and Henri de Lubac,[5] were both Jesuits. Among the spirituality traditions, the legacy of Ignatius of Loyola is one that particularly values the knowlege of the redemptive process that comes from reflection on personal experience.

Yet it is also true that the same thrust has come from other currents in modern culture. It is a logical outcome of the Enlightenment, which asserted in a general way the authority of reason over the authority of tradition and hierarchic status. The Modernist movement anticipated, in ways that could not at that time be accepted, the work of the twentieth century Catholic theologians that became normative for the Second Vatican Council. In the twentieth century the philosophical movements of existentialism and phenomenology have had an influence that really pervaded all dimensions of western thought. The existentialist current swept through the New Testament studies of Rudolf Bultmann[6] and others into the monumental Protestant systematic theology of Paul Tillich[7], whose soteriology and Christology were all part of a tightly knit synthesis of Christian doctrines based on one aspect of human experience, namely the introspective experience of the single individual. This same existentialist trend, of course, influenced Karl Rahner in his perception and reformulation of soteriology and Christology.[8]

---

[4]*op. cit.*

[5]*op. cit.*

[6]See, for instance, *Jesus Christ and Mythology*, Rudolf Bultmann, (N.Y.: Scribners, 1958), and the collection, *Existence and Faith, Shorter Writings of Rudolf Bultmann*, Selected and translated by Schubert M. Ogden (N.Y.: Meridian, 1950).

[7]*Systematic Theology*, 3 Volumes, (Chicago: University of Chicago Press, 1963).

[8]*Cf.* the series of essays on this subject matter in *Theological Investigations*: and *Foundations of Christian Faith* (N.Y.: Seabury, 1978), Part VI.

Yet there has been a strong sense that these formulations did not entirely answer the question. The philosophical movement of phenomenology suggested the consideration of a broader sweep of experience than the individual introspective. It has led to the inter-personal analysis of experience in the soteriology and Christology of Schillebeeckx[9] and in a lesser way of Walter Kasper.[10] At the same time, the content rather than the method of soteriology and Christology has been strongly influenced by evolutionary and process thought, asserting within theology something important about the shape and texture of all contemporary experience, namely its sense of definition with reference to the future. This has given a further critical dimension to the soteriology and Christology of Schoonenberg,[11] Pannenberg,[12] and Moltmann,[13] a dimension that is pressed to the extreme in some authors such as John B. Cobb.[14]

In all of this, however, there remains a conspicuous common bias. It rather consistently avoids the political and economic dimension of human experience. It makes little connection between the notion of salvation in Jesus Christ and the felt needs of salvation of the vast masses of humankind, whose hunger for fulfilment is in the first place an urgent

[9]This is made particularly explicit in *Jesus, an Experiment in Christology*, E. Schillebeeckx (N.Y.: Seabury, 1979), Part I.

[10]*Jesus the Christ* (N.Y.: Paulist, 1976).

[11]See *The Christ* (N.Y.: Herder, 1971) and a series of subsequent articles, *e.g.* those listed in footnote 27 below and those in footnote 6, Chapter 3 of the present volume.

[12]*op. cit.*

[13]*Cf. The Crucified God* (N.Y.: Harper & Row, 1974.)

[14]*Christ in a Pluralistic Age* (Philadelphia: Westminster, 1975).

hunger for physical sustenance and whose yearning for fulness of life is in the first place an anxiety about physical survival from day to day. It is at this juncture that the plea arises, mainly from Third World liberation theologians, for a soteriology and Christology that are concerned not only with contemporary experience of believers as interacting individuals but with the entire range of human experience of suffering and hoping and surviving and transformation, which includes the political and economic dimensions of human life.

Out of this have come the theologies, sharply focussed on soteriology, of Gustavo Gutierrez,[15] Rubem Alves,[16] Rene Laurentin,[17] Hugo Assmann,[18] Jose Miguez Bonino,[19] Ignacio Ellacuria,[20] Enrique Dussel,[21] Julio de Santa Ana,[22] Paolo Arturi,[23] Jose Maria Gonzalez-Ruiz,[24] Juan Luis Segundo,[25] and others. All of these theologies, however, are hampered by the lack of a Christology consistent with the demands of the soteriology proposed. The main preoccupation of these

[15]*A Theology of Liberation* (Maryknoll, N.Y .: Orbis, 1973).

[16]*A Theology of Human Hope* (Washington: Corpus, 1970).

[17]*Liberation, Development and Salvation* (Maryknoll, N.Y.: Orbis, 1972).

[18]*Theology for a Nomad Church* (Maryknoll, N.Y.: Orbis, 1976).

[19]*Doing Theology in a Revolutionary Situation* (Philadelphia: Fortress, 1975).

[20]*Freedom Made Flesh* (Maryknoll, N.Y.: Orbis, 1976).

[21]*History and the Theology of Liberation* (Maryknoll, N.Y.: Orbis, 1976).

[22]*Good News to the Poor* (Maryknoll, N.Y.: Orbis, 1979).

[23]*Freedom to be Free* (Maryknoll, N.Y.: Orbis, 1973).

[24]*The New Creation: Marxist and Christian?* (Maryknoll, N.Y.: Orbis, 1976).

[25]*Theology for Artisans of a New Humanity*, 5 Volumes, especially Vol. 2, *Grace and the Human Condition* (N.Y., Maryknoll: Orbis, 1973). It is noteworthy, however, that there is no Christology at all in this five volume series.

authors is to discern in the complex human situation of our times the true relationships between the various kinds of freedom that human persons seek, and particularly the way in which all other kinds of liberation relate to liberation from sin and reconciliation with God. In keeping with this concern, Ignacio Ellacuria has suggested, but not elaborated further, a Christology based on Jesus as freedom incarnate to be identified with the *logos* of the classic Christologies but with the important difference that *logos* is understood by Ellacuria as having an historical dimension[26] — a point which had already been made by Schoonenberg.[27] The proposal to interpret Jesus as divine freedom incarnate had, of course, been made earlier by Nicolai Berdyaev, in a sense which combined the political and existential aspects of freedom in human history,[28] and the possibilities which Berdyaev's work opened up seem not to have been explored sufficiently in subsequent western Christian theology.

Two Latin American liberation theologians have carried the question concerning the difference that Jesus makes in human history into a systematic constructive Christology. Leonardo Boff in a work first published in Portuguese in 1972,[29] moves from historical inquiry through a soteriological consideration into the traditional Christological questions

[26]*op. cit.* , pp. 24-27.

[27]*E.g.* "Process or History in God?," *Louvain Studies* 4, pp. 303-319, Fall 1973; "Chalcedon and Divine Immutability," *Theology Digest* 29, pp. 103-107, Summer 1981.

[28]*Freedom and Spirit,* quoted at length in *Christian Existentialism,* a Berdyaev anthology selected and translated by Donald A. Lowrie (N.Y.: Harper and Row, 1965) pp. 51-52.

[29]The English translation, *Jesus Christ, the Liberator,* was published by Orbis in 1978 with an epilogue added which expanded the political references in a way not possible in the Portuguese of 1972.

concerning the identity of Jesus in relation to the human and the divine. Disappointingly, however, the concluding section which deals with Christology, proceeds not from the foregoing soteriological reflections (according to the liberation theologians' understanding that theology is always reflection on the praxis of the Christian life) but, without further ado, directly from the classic dogmatic formulations.[30]

Jon Sobrino, in a work published first in Spanish in 1976, was able to carry the process of reflection and formulation further.[31] He sets up criteria for a method in Christology,[32] which will largely be followed in the constructive section of the present volume, whereby the Christology may truly be coherent with the soteriological context in which it is formulated. He also offers a systematic elaboration on the foundation of these criteria,[33] though one which becomes very sketchy as it moves into the final questions concerning the identity of Jesus, and leaves what seem to be unintended ambiguities. In spite of this, Sobrino offers a very helpful contemporary approach to the question concerning the difference that Jesus makes. The present volume is an attempt to carry the same line of inquiry further into a constructive Christology.

---

[30]*ibid.* Ch.10.

[31]*Christology at the Crossroads*, published in English by Maryknoll in 1978. Originally *Cristologia desde América Latina.*

[32]*ibid.* Chs. 1, 2 and 11.

[33]*ibid., passim.* More particularly, Chapters 10 and 11 offer a critique of conventional Christology and some "theses" for the development of a new Christology, but these are not further elaborated. For instance, the divinity claim is not fully explained, though parameters for such an explanation are set out.

The broad question concerning the difference that Jesus makes gives rise in the context of the traditional teachings to some very specific Christian questions: why should Jesus be considered the single and universal mediator-savior? What are his qualifications for this role? and what is the present relationship of the believer to Jesus? Whereas the general question of the difference Jesus makes is a question that might also be proposed by non-Christians, as it was undoubtedly by Gandhi for instance, these more specific questions arise for the Christian because of the traditional formulations that have been taught authoritatively and have shaped Christian identity and consciousness.

In the contemporary world, with its almost universal experience of cultural and religious plurality, even firmly committed Christians must sometimes ask questions concerning the claims made for the uniqueness of Jesus. There must have been long ages of Christendom in which the universal significance and saving power of Jesus of Nazareth could indeed be taken for granted. Actual political and social experience appeared to verify the Christian teachings. The known civilized world was indeed drawn together in the Christian faith, though there was always the scandal of schisms great and small. Moreover, an almost exclusive focus on salvation to be attained beyond death must surely have softened the impact of social injustices and cruelties upon the credibility of Christendom. Jews were relatively few and easily — too easily —accounted for by a negative theological explanation. Muslims were peripheral and rather easily dismissed as "infidels." All who were seen as normal by most Christian believers were embraced within the Christian Church and culture and policy in a symbiosis that must have seemed more or less inevitable and self-validating.

Since the era of the great colonizations, the rise of modern science and technology and consequent increased travel and communication, and perhaps most of all since the intellectual movement of the Enlightenment, the experience of Christendom has vanished. It has been replaced by an experience of plurality, that is by an experience that nothing in one's own culture and tradition can be taken for granted. Large, and sometimes universal claims of salvation are also made by other faiths, for instance the Muslim and the Buddhist and the Bahai. To point out, along the lines of our traditional Christian apologetic, that none make exactly the personal claims for a great leader that Christians make, is simply beside the point. It is precisely the contention of these faiths that by the nature of ultimate reality as we can know it and by the nature of the human person, the kind of claim which Christians make for Jesus is misleading and not truly liberating or salvific.

What this asks of Christians — and this has, of course, always been true of apologetics — is not the formulation of a response that will convince and convert the others, but the more rigorous quest within the experience and vision of Christian believers for that understanding which makes the Christian faith intellectually coherent and practically self-validating for Christians themselves. Nor can this be achieved by showing inconsistencies or anomalies in the other traditions, as though by a process of elimination that could somehow justify one's own. The kind of understanding for which contemporary Christians are searching is one that justifies itself in terms of the experience in which they themselves participate — the whole human experience in its social and individual, its public and its private, its avowedly secular and its explicitly religious dimensions.

Increasingly since the nineteenth century, the challenge to the Christian believer has come from Marxist thought, Marxist political protest and Marxist political experimentation. Precisely because our representation of salvation has become more and more ethereal, more and more other-worldly, less and less responsive to urgent, all-consuming present suffering, degradation, dehumanization, there is great cogency in the Marxist question and answer about human salvation. Furthermore, precisely because our Christian expectation of salvation has not always been like this, but originated in a biblical expectation that was inclusive of both spiritual and earthly concrete concerns, the cogency of the Marxist question raises answering echoes in Christian consciousness. This is not something that is happening at the fringes of Christian community and faith but at the center. It is not the ignorant but those who know the scriptures and the tradition well, who are deeply affected by this challenge. Likewise it is not those marginally committed to their Christian faith, but rather those who are generously dedicated in a life of radical renunciations, who most frequently experience the penetration of the Marxist question.

It is this, of course, that has been most influential in directing the quest for the historical Jesus into political and socio-historical, socio-critical channels. It is this that has provoked the struggle to formulate a Latin American liberation theology attempting to recover the totality of Christian soteriology. And out of this same challenge have come the efforts to look again at Christology in the narrower sense of the term, searching for ways of identifying Jesus with reference to the divine, the human and the redemptive task.

In this context, the urgent task is not so much to demonstrate that Jesus is the one and universal mediator of salvation, as to discover the dimensions of the saving effects in our Christian experience that lead us to recognize the basic human validity and universal applicability of what we have experienced. It is a task that is bound to be somewhat more difficult, subtle and complex now than it was for preachers of the apostolic age or Greek apologists of the second century, not only because of the passage of time and the growth in numbers but also because mass conversions and experiences of establishment have brought about a general confusion of the specifically Christian with the cultural and political traditions dominant in the West.

What we need to do now is to rediscover those qualities of the teaching, life-style, relationships, impact, death and post-Resurrection effect of Jesus which constitute his saving role. We need to consider openly and critically how, where, on whom, and why Jesus has had and is having an impact, and how this reshapes human memory and imagination, human experience and action and hope. This, of course, is intimately intertwined with the question concerning the relationship of the believer to Jesus in the present. It is simply not possible to answer questions about the impact of Jesus from a detached viewpoint and to arrive at a theological explanation adequate to the contemporary believer's need. The information we have about Jesus in person is both sketchy and stylized, and is deliberately left open to further developments of understanding in the dialogue of that early testimony with the faith and experience of succeeding generations of followers of Jesus.

2

Where the Traditional Symbolism
Hinders

It is clear that Scripture offers us many images, symbols, analogies by which to attempt to approach an understanding of the person and the significance of Jesus. Some of these were simply dropped, some were used and elaborated into a Christology for some time and then fell into disuse,[1] some have continued to be used in worship but have not really been used for theological explanations or arguments, and a few have become the normative basis for all theological discussion. Recent attempts to make the person and significance of Jesus more intelligible to Christian believers, have turned to the

[1]See, e.g., the study of these in James D.G. Dunn, *Christology in the Making* (Philadelphia: Westminster, 1980) *passim.* and *cf.* Frans Jozef van Beeck, *Christ Proclaimed: Christology as Rhetoric* (N.Y.: Paulist, 1979), Ch.4.

forgotten or neglected themes and titles in Scripture. Helpful as these have been, no Christology that bypasses the Council of Chalcedon and the vocabulary and imagery there established, is likely to be taken seriously by communities of believers other than those committed to an extreme interpretation of the principle, *sola scriptura*.[2]

To be taken seriously in most Christian churches today, any attempt at Christology must establish its orthodoxy for the community of believers by explaining its congruence with Chalcedon. This in itself is not a problem. What constitutes a problem is that for many centuries we not only offered Christologies that could be shown to be in harmony with Chalcedon, but we really restricted ourselves to further elaboration and refinement of the categories of Chalcedon, and we retained the vocabulary even when the meaning commonly conveyed by the terms drifted rather far afield. Even this, of course, need not have presented a great problem if that vocabulary had been used only among professional theologians and if these professional theologians had been aware throughout the centuries of the phenomenon of semantic drift and of the particular history of the Christological arguments and their formulations. In fact, neither of these conditions was fulfilled. For centuries the history of the doctrinal formulations was very little known or appreciated and vocabulary was used as though meaning were static through changing times and cultures.

The problem with the retention of the Chalcedonian vocabulary and the restriction of Christological argument

---

[2]The Chalcedonian debate is not repeated here. See, *e.g.* Richard A. Norris, *The Christological Controversy* (Philadelphia: Fortress, 1980), especially Ch.IX.

within the categories of Chalcedon is a complex human one. The formulations were quite generally used in catechesis and preaching and devotional writing as well as in professional theological argumentation. Therefore even among theologians, these terms had become familiar long before there was any awareness of the frame of reference within which they were to be understood. There can be little doubt that to most Christians for some centuries, speaking of Three Persons in One God was simply synonymous with naming three people each of whom and all of whom were to be regarded as God. In fact, it would probably be seen as a technical quibble that one was not supposed to speak of three Gods; that was just not the right formula, though most would be hard put to it to explain why. Likewise for most Christians, to say that in Christ there are two natures and one person, with the emphasis on the assumption that the one person, along with one of the natures, was divine while the other nature was human, was simply to say that Jesus was a God disguised or, as it were, bewitched, into human form, more or less on the analogy of the frog-prince or the swan-maidens and such.

This is, of course, diametrically opposed to the intent of Chalcedon which was before all else concerned with a defense of the true humanity of Jesus, for it was that full humanity, and not the divinity claim, that was under dispute. Yet the effect of the retention and the widespread use of this language concerning the person and natures of Christ, has been to turn Jesus into an alien among us who spent a little while in exile for our sake and then left our planet and mode of existence again to return to his "own proper" sphere.

The further difficulty then emerges that not only is Jesus an alien among us (and as such not really imitable) but his significance for the redemption of the world is also rather clearly quite independent of anything that he ever did in the world. His character as universal mediator of salvation is already assured by his prior divine identity, yielding a Christology in which the doctrine of the Incarnation renders life, preaching, passion, death and resurrection all rather peripheral to the significance of Jesus, that is, to the difference that he makes in the history of the human community. This is a severe problem to Christian believers because they consider themselves followers or imitators of Jesus. It suggests that the perfect model of what is human before God is that of inactivity. If the redemptive event was that the human nature of Jesus was assumed by the divine prior to any human decision, then it is reasonable to conclude that one becomes party to the redemption rather simply by being taken (baptized) into the realm of the divine Jesus, the realm of grace, prior to any human decision or response. Anything that follows in lifestyle, action, personal commitment and so forth would tend to be peripheral. Christian lives and actions might be much the same as those of unbelievers, but that would not be important because the essential difference has been made even though no change may be apparent.

This is, of course, a rather simplistic and caricatured account of the attitudes and their connection with Christology,[3] yet the contemporary discomfort with the conventional symbolism of Christology seems to be based on the discovery of this connection. It seems that the cumulative effect of our

---

[3]For a fuller analysis of the connection between Christologies and social attitudes see Monika Hellwig, "Christology and Attitudes towards Social Structures," in *Above Every Name: the Lordship of Christ and Social Systems*, ed. Thomas E. Clarke (N.Y.: Paulist, 1980), pp.13-34.

Christology as commonly understood and assimilated is to suggest that whatever is significant with reference to the redemption happens prior to human decision and human creativity. That is why the Marxist question carries so much weight: what redemption, what salvation is it really of which Christians speak? But the problem is almost insoluble if soteriology is derived from Christology and that Christology is restricted within the language and analogies of Chalcedon.

The popular misconceptions and their consequences seem to hamper professional theologians also. No one is born a professional theologian and no one becomes a professional theologian prior to assimilating the language and piety and perceptions of the Christian community, along with its misconceptions. For centuries theologians have had to try to unlearn some false and inaccurate understandings in order to try to approach the meaning of Jesus. In itself this is no easy task even in an age in which we are well aware of semantic drift and and in which the history of doctrines has been uncovered and made generally available. It must have been far more difficult in times when the historical dimension of human thought and culture was not evident.

The manner in which questions have been considered and problems have arisen in our conventional Christology suggests that a naive interpretation of the word "person" in the trinitarian and Christological doctrines has unnecessarily complicated the issues. The discussions, for instance, concerning the knowledge of Jesus and his awareness of his identity, suggest that Persons in the godhead were implicitly taken to mean three separate reflectively self-aware centers of consciousness, relating to one another and knowing and willing in some manner closely analogous to our own relating, knowing and willing. Likewise, the oft noted anxiety to escape heresy by tortuous circumlocutions enabling one to avoid referring to Jesus as a human person, obviously implied the understanding that divine Person, as used in the classic doctrinal formulations, and human person, as used in common speech, were comparable items in a common category and known to be mutually exclusive but exchangeable.

Of course, each generation of theologians has wrestled with the problem of extricating the traditional doctrine from the misconceptions, and in our own generation there has been much scholarly research into the biblical foundations of Christology, the early historical development, and the dogmatic parameters which history has left us. Yet the amount of energy and ingenuity that has gone into this shows that the traditional symbolism that is circumscribed by the formulations of Chalcedon often hinders more than it helps piety and understanding. This is not surprising, for that traditional symbolism is based upon alien experience, alien culture and alien philosophy. Contemporary understanding can surely build bridges to meet this alien formulation, but it cannot build bridges from this alien formulation as the starting point. We proceed in understanding from the known to the unknown, from what lies within our experience to what lies beyond it.

The Chalcedonian formulations include, of course, the Nicene creed as modified at Constantinople, the statement of Ephesus, two letters of Cyril of Alexandria, the Tome of Leo the Great, as well as the confession of faith of the Council of Chalcedon itself.[4] These documents are firmly rooted in the

---

[4] *Cf.* Norris, *op. cit,* Ch.IX, and J.N.D. Kelly, *Early Christian Doctrines* (N.Y.: Harper & Row, 1958), especially Ch.XII.

liturgical and devotional formulae of the time as well as in the development of doctrine up to that time. All the authors were concerned with appropriate language and imagery for the instruction of adult converts to Christian faith. More particularly, this language and imagery had to be appropriate for the reshaping of pagan consciousness, worldview, identity and focus in life, into a Christian consciousness, worldview, identity and focus in life. For this purpose it was neither necessary nor possible to challenge the cosmology, anthropology or total ontology through which the Greek-speaking world of the fourth and fifth centuries interpreted its experience and expressed its yearnings. And indeed the authors who contributed to the formulations of Chalcedon attempted to give the rationale of Christian hope by explaining the significance of Jesus precisely within those categories which must have appeared to Christians of that time to be the categories of inescapable common sense reality and experience.

In spite of excellent contemporary historical research, that experience of the fading pagan world of late antiquity remains largely quite inaccessible to us. Most of all, the lived experience of participating in the debates that led to these formulations can never be ours. They are necessarily debates long past and settled, which arose out of the experience of other people long dead, with concerns long forgotten. Because the process of formulating can never be ours, the finished formulation is never quite ours. It is inevitably alien in that sense. But this is not all.

It is not only the actual participation that fails us. The formulations are the expressions of a culture that is also entirely foreign to us. It is difficult for us even to imagine life in late antiquity — the sense of time and of the possibility of the timeless, the distribution of roles in society by sex and birth and other predetermining factors, the perception of what is central in human life and what is peripheral, the implicit factors on which identity was based, the experience of the sacred in its pagan and in its Christian expressions. In short, Christians of the fourth and fifth centuries asked and answered some questions which we have great difficulty not so much in understanding as in taking seriously. These debates and the solutions found for them do not seem to address questions that are critical for us in coming to an understanding of the meaning of Jesus — questions such as the relation of Jesus to political, economic, racial and psychological freedom, questions such as the finality of Jesus in relation to other great religious movements and traditions, and so forth.

The problem is most acute, as has long been noted, in relation to the philosophical background of the Chalcedonian formulations.[5] Philosophy may seem to be a concern of a few leisured specialists whose experience and thoughts are rather remote from the practical concerns of the rest of the community. But this is in fact not so at all. Philosophers reflect on the experience in which they share, and they only gain a hearing and become known to the rest of us to the extent that they speak and write of something that they truly share and which we recognize as our experience. Moreover, they only become successful if the structure that they give to our experience by their thought seems to the rest of us to make sense and to aid understanding. There is a complex and subtle reciprocity between the popularly diffused sense of pattern and meaning

---

[5] *Cf.* Leslie Dewart, *The Future of Belief* (N.Y.: Herder, 1966) and the review of it by Bernard Lonergan in *Theological Studies*, June 1967, Vol. 28, pp. 336-351.

in the reality of our experience on the one hand and the disciplined intellectual effort of specialists to formulate and interpret it on the other hand. Successful philosophies are in tune with the widely diffused popular view of common sense reality.

In our own times, the meaning and the connotations carried by the word, *logos*, both inside and outside the Christian Christological discussions, are simply not part of our perception or interpretation of reality. The word, person, is used for an individual of the human species, allowing for the possibility that there might exist somewhere other species whose individuals we should also consider as persons in recognition of the quality of their consciousness (as rational and reflexive), their capacity for relationships and the creativity of their impact on their environment. Nature as we understand it, is not an entirely static reality either in its global sense or in its individual realization. We do not think of the "really real" as being outside of time and space and impervious to change. All of these factors and many more mean that we cannot find the meaning of Jesus by beginning with Chalcedon[6] and trying somehow to adapt it to a more contemporary expression.

Yet the Church is in some sense committed to Chalcedon as an enduring reference point, a criterion of orthodoxy. It seems as though we are caught between the horns of the dilemma. However, the dilemma is only apparent. Chalcedon became, early in Christian history, the criterion of orthodoxy for all Christological expressions — liturgical, devotional,

---

[6]Cf. An early essay by Karl Rahner, "Current Problems in Christology" in *Theological Investigations*, vol. 1 (Baltimore, Helicon, 1961) pp. 149-200.

doctrinal. It is not, and has never been, the primary source for Christology. The primary source for Christology is the historical and risen Jesus as experienced and testified by the community of believers from the beginning. And the solution to the apparent dilemma is in the constant return to the source, through the sources. If Chalcedon, as the voice of the Church assembled in the Spirit, speaks the truth of Christology, then any quest that sets out anew from the sources should find its reconciliation with Chalcedon at the end, though this final reconciliation need not be explicit from the beginning in the vocabulary and categories and style of argumentation used.

3

Return to the Sources

It is quite clear that an effective Christology must constantly return to the sources and must truly recognize and acknowledge the sources. Our theory is, in fact, always a critical reflection on our praxis, our Christian theology a critical reflection on our life and prayer as Christians. This is so whether or not we acknowledge it or are even aware of it. Yet the quality of any theory, and of theology in particular, is markedly different when this is acknowledged and when it is not. To acknowledge one's theology as critical reflection on Christian life and worship means, in the first place, to be open to change. The logic of an argument may come to an incontrovertible conclusion and the authoritative pronouncement of an official source may be beyond further question, but reflection on life and worship does not simply come to a permanent conclusion, for life and worship continue in ever new insights, challenges and outcomes.

Even more importantly, perhaps, acknowledging one's theology as critical reflection on Christian life and worship means expecting and accepting plurality of expression. When the reality of Christian life and worship is experienced differently by different communities, traditions or individuals, this does not necessarily mean a conflict of truth claims. More frequently it offers a complementarity in truth claims. And viewing the matter thus, one expects variety and complementarity in the expressions that arise from critical reflection upon varied experiences. This is the normal outcome and the usual and acceptable state of affairs. Only by way of rare exception should it be necessary to force a confrontation and debate of positions and formulations in order to arrive at a uniform, normative expression.

This, indeed, seems to have been the situation in the early church. The New Testament, as modern scholarship has clearly shown, offers a wide spectrum of Christologies which none of the authors tries to fuse into one.[1] This is hardly surprising. In the absence of an established official Christology at that early stage, those who preached and wrote and those who listened and read must all have been aware that what they were doing was a critical reflection on their lives and their changed outlook as followers of Jesus, crucified and risen. For some centuries this awareness is still evident in the extant writings. Even in such very speculative writings as some of Origen's works, it is quite clear that the authors are aware of their own creative initiatives to reflect on their Christian lives and to give expression to that reflection in categories of

---

[1]See James D.G. Dunn, *Christology in the Making* (Philadelphia: Westminster, 1980), "Conclusion," pp. 248-268.

thought sufficiently established and diffused to be able to convey some sense of their own understanding to their contemporaries.

Although the great Councils of the fourth and fifth centuries seem to have been required more by the needs of the emperors to tidy things up administratively in the churches, than by the spontaneous needs for communion of language and thought in the Christian community, the participants still seem to have been aware of drawing their theology from reflections on their Christian experience. It is true that there was little tolerance for the variety of local church traditions. The spirit and expectation of that time of imperial consolidation seemed to be against such tolerance. Yet the appeal, in Leo's Tome for instance, is an appeal to all Christians of his time to reflect on their own prayers, on their experience of catechumenate and initiation, on the profession of faith commonly made by Christians, and on their Christian way of life. Likewise, the symbol of faith formally adopted at Nicea and Constantinople had been drawn from the confession used in worship in the initiation process, which in turn used traditional expressions of the impact that Jesus had made on his followers and their understanding of his history and identity in terms of that impact.

After the age of the great Councils, however, there appears to have been a subtle shift — one that is not unusual in the history of a great tradition. It was a shift from theology seen primarily as reflection on the praxis of Christian life and worship, to theology seen primarily as reflection on doctrinal formulations passed on from earlier generations. The tacit assumption underlying this was that these earlier generations were closer to the source of the truth and better placed to make dogmatic statements as well as giving interpretations. This began to apply not only to the witnesses of the apostolic and sub-apostolic age, who were presumed to have had direct or close indirect contact with the historical Jesus and the original events of the resurrection, but also to the ancients in a very broad sweep of centuries — what we should call the patristic era.

It need hardly be said that in this assumption lay the seed of alienation of the theological process from the lived experience of the Christian communities. It did not happen all at once. While theology was going on mainly in the monasteries and in the cathedral schools it was still very clearly prayerful reflection on the Christian life and faith of the authors and on their pastoral tasks in many cases. As the pattern of cathedral schools gave way to that of universities (that is, of corporations of scholars) this could no longer be claimed. Theology became a professional field alongside of medicine and law, and a strong element of competition entered between schools and between leading scholars. Scholasticism is a very different way of doing theology, far more directly governed by the kinds of logical and rhetorical rules that pertain in academic debate than by breadth of life experience, piety or poetic insight. The participation of the friars, many of whom were undoubtedly truly holy men and most of whom were very pastorally minded, may have alleviated this in some measure but it could not turn the tide. The soteriological and Christological debates and writings of the mediaeval period bear ample witness to this fact.

It would not be accurate to think that therefore theology stood still at this time and was confined to the wooden repetition of past formulations. Nothing could be further from the truth. It was a period of feverish theological activity. The work of Thomas Aquinas alone, so little recognized in his own time in the midst of all the scholastic activity, shows enormous creativity. Moreover the *auctoritates* that were cited so abundantly in scholastic argumentation were not given as conclusions or preordained answers but as starting points for the reflection. Yet the fact remains that these *auctoritates* rather than observations from the lived contemporary experience were the sources from which the theological discussion drew its content.

In this respect the Protestant Reformation and its Catholic counterparts did not really help much. In spite of Luther's much discussed personal, experiential foundation for his thought, the long term effect of the Reformation on western theology, both Protestant and Catholic, appears to have been rather to focus attention even more sharply on authoritative source texts of each sub-tradition and to direct the theological discussion into defense of positions based on those source texts. Nineteenth century thought turned away from source texts other than the Bible in many cases, but it was largely in favor of reason and scientific investigation. Only, perhaps, with the romantic movement was there more inclination to take present experience of believers seriously.

It was left to the twentieth century to turn around full circle and acknowledge the role of contemporary believers' experience as a source for our understanding in Christology. Karl Rahner made this explicit in principle when he began to write of "an inquiring Christology" as something that is happening wherever human persons are sincerely searching for the meaning of human life, especially in terms of accepting and responding to freedom, death and others.[2] Rahner also approached the same realization in slightly different terms when he wrote about an *a priori* and an *a posteriori* approach to Christology — what we *can* be talking about, what *can* be at issue, what it *can* mean, on the one hand, and what the witnesses do in fact testify on the other.[3] The same author has suggested a kind of hermeneutic circle: while it is true that all theology is anthropology (as Feuerbach maintained), it is also true that Christian anthropology is Christology.[4]

These several approaches proposed by Karl Rahner were widely accepted and quite influential because they were in harmony with the general awakening of more explicit self-awareness which expressed itself in the existentialist movement in thought. There was also, however, a different and complementary thought movement, looking out into the world rather than in towards human consciousness. This movement, sparked no doubt by developments in science and technology, has been characterized by awareness of constant change, continuing growth, unending development, process. It focussed on the evolutionary character of the universe, and it hailed the philosopher Whitehead and the Jesuit scientist-mystic Teilhard de Chardin among its spokesmen. In this movement the Christian experience out of which all theology including Christology arose was an evolutionary experience. Christology also was considered in terms of becoming, in

---

[2]See *Foundations of Christian Faith* (N.Y.: Seabury, 1978) Ch.VI, for a retrospective synthesis.

[3]*ibid*

[4]"Theology and Anthropology," in T. Patrick Burke, ed., *The Word in History* (N.Y.: Sheed & Ward, 1966) pp. 1-23.

terms of continuing evolution within human history. Teilhard led the way with his contemporary and scientifically situated vision of Christ as the *omega* point of human (and of all) evolution, realized in ultimate and intimate universal human community.[5] His vision is essentially that already expressed in the letters to the Colossians and Ephesians of the New Testament. It had been developed in ways appropriate to another age by Theodore of Mopsuestia. But it had a freshness that carried great conviction for our own times in the manner in which the imagery was developed by Teilhard.

This evolutionary or process mode of interpretation has influenced many of the contemporary Christologies, such as the very profound series of christological writings of Piet Schoonenberg.[6] Even Karl Rahner, with his established existentialist perspective, found himself obliged to respond to the call for an evolutionary Christology.[7] This has been an important movement in theology, largely because it has recaptured the sense that all creation is essentially holy and that our relationship with God is not a private and individual matter but rather is one that permeates all human activities including

[5]See, Teilhard de Chardin, *The Phenomenon of Man* (N.Y.: Harper & Row, 1959), "Epilogue," pp. 291-296, and *Christianity and Evolution* (N.Y.: Harcourt Brace, 1971) *passim.*

[6]Some sense of the progression of the thought of Piet Schoonenberg, is available in English in: "He Emptied Himself — Philippians 2.7," in *Who is Jesus of Nazareth?* ed. Edward Schillebeeckx and Bonifaas Willems (N.Y.: Paulist, 1965); *The Christ* (N.Y.: Herder, 1971) which was the translation of *Hij is een God van Mensen* (published in Dutch in 1969); "God's presence in Jesus: exchange of viewpoints," in *Theology Digest* 19, spring 1971. pp. 29-38; "Process or History in God?," in *Louvain Studies*, 4, Fall 1973, pp. 303-319; "Spirit Christology and Logos Christology," in *Bijdragen* 38, 1977, pp. 350-375.; "From a Two-Nature Christology to a Christology of Presence," in *Theological Folia of Villanova University*, Speculative Studies, vol II, 1975, pp. 219-243.

[7]See, "Christology Within an Evolutionary View of the World," in *Theological Investigations*, vol. V, (Baltimore: Helicon, 1966) pp. 157-193.

scientific and technical progress and adaptation, and including all the practical complexity of modern life. In doing this, the evolutionary mode of interpretation helped to overcome the alienation of our theology from our own contemporary experience. It allowed contemporary experience to become a source for theological reflection precisely in those dimensions that seemed most profane.

However, particularly in Christology, this still left a gap that many Christians felt to be unbridgeable. It seemed that an evolutionary Christology must always be somehow triumphalist; it appears to assume that essentially the world we know is the redeemed world with minor flaws that will be corrected by the inherent process of history. An evolutionary Christology seems from the outset to envisage redemption from the perspective of established values and social structures, because it tends to assume that what is is better than what was and to stress that the germ of redemption is in the whole unfolding human history. The becoming of the whole Christ tends to be seen as simply identical with the process of history while the conflictual aspect of incarnation, resurrection and *parousia* is de-emphasized.

In spite of suggestions in that direction derived from the thought of Hegel, most theologians have rejected a purely evolutionary or process formulation of Christology as inadequate in accounting for the scandal of the cross and the mystery of the crucified and risen Jesus. This was an appeal not so much to contemporary experience as to classic formulations. Yet, at the same time, other voices began to be heard that did speak from their own contemporary experience. They spoke of suffering, systematic oppression, exclusion from the

process of history, destitution and hunger, terror and hopelessness. And they claimed that the meaning of Jesus as Lord and
Savior could be understood in contemporary terms precisely
out of these experiences of suffering and of deprivation of
hope.

From these cries there arose first a series of short-lived
attempts at revolutionary rather than evolutionary theologies
and later a steady stream of writings on "liberation theology."[8]
This term, which was used by Latin American authors since
1970, describes a movement in Christian theology of the
West, both Catholic and Protestant. The movement is concerned to recover the understanding that Christian theology is
reflection on the experience of Christian life, that among the
followers of the crucified the experience of the poor, the
oppressed and the rejected is privileged experience for such
reflection, and that redemption or liberation from sin is
concerned with all aspects of human life and with all the
structures of human society that crush or disable people.

Liberation theology was at first nothing more than an
appeal that theology should be done in this way, using the
experience of the poor and oppressed as a source for reflection.[9] Later it began to offer some attempts at constructive
theologies,[10] yet those for the most part lacked a Christology
— a lack which their authors freely acknowledged, claiming
that the time was not ripe for it, that the attempts at constructive theology along liberation theology lines were not yet

[8]*Cf.* footnotes 14 - 24, Ch. 1

[9]Such as the early works of Miguez-Bonino, Assmann and Dussel.

[10]*e.g. Freedom Made Flesh* by Ignacio Ellacuria (Maryknoll: Orbis, 1976) is such an
attempt focussing particularly on ecclesiology.

mature enough to produce a Christology. Nevertheless liberation theology stands or falls according to whether it is able to offer a coherent Christology according to its own criteria. Those criteria are really three: to approach the meaning of Jesus out of the experience of a Christian struggle for the liberation of the oppressed; to be true to the New Testament testimonies concerning the historical Jesus and the faith of his early followers; and, finally, to offer a soteriology and Christology in harmony with classic Christian tradition, particularly the formulations of Chalcedon.

There have been many books on Jesus within the frame of reference of a liberation theology, but they have not been Christologies for the most part.[11] That is to say, they have more usually been only one step towards a Christology. They have been concerned to reconsider the testimonies we have concerning the historical Jesus, putting those testimonies in the context of their historical, social and political setting. They have labored to "de-privatize" our modern perception of the original testimonies by showing the social and political and even powerfully revolutionary implications of the words and actions of Jesus presented in the New Testament. For most Christians this is perhaps the more important part of the task, because its implications for Christian attitudes, actions and expectations are immediate and crucial. Being a follower of Jesus is a very different matter if his gospel had and has strong revolutionary connotations for the social, economic and political structures by which people's lives are made and marred.

[11]Examples are: Segundo Galilea, *Following Jesus* (Maryknoll: Orbis, 1981); *Jesus before Christianity* by Albert Nolan, (Maryknoll: Orbis 1978); Richard J. Cassidy, *Jesus, Politics and Society* (Maryknoll: Orbis, 1978).; Sebastian Kappen, *Jesus and Freedom* (Maryknoll: Orbis, 1977)

What the following of Jesus has meant in the more populous churches in modern times has more usually assumed the strict separation of religious faith from public affairs. Only direct persecution of Christians, or the implementation of policies contrary to explicit church teachings, have broken into this assumption of the privacy of the faith and its implications for living.

Among the many books on Jesus written from the perspective of contemporary struggles for human liberation, there are two which have offered a constructive Christology, moving beyond the depicting of the historical Jesus and his teachings, actions, life-style and impact, to consider also the classic questions of Christology and to offer solutions in harmony with the classic tradition. These are the studies by Leonardo Boff[12] and by Jon Sobrino.[13] Both these authors accept the formulations of Chalcedon, but approach the meaning of these formulations from the contemporary experience of the oppressed and the soteriological questions that arise from that experience. Boff juxtaposes the plurality of titles given to Jesus in the New Testament with a plurality of titles arising out of contemporary experience and tries to show that the wording of Chalcedon, rightly understood, comprehends and transcends them all in the breadth of its claim (which makes it the classic statement) while at the same time failing to address crucial questions (which makes it an insufficient basis for a Christology).[14]

---

[12]*Jesus Christ, Liberator* (N.Y.: Orbis, 1978). The original Portuguese version had been published in 1972.

[13]*Christology at the Crossroads* (N.Y.: Orbis, 1978). The original Spanish version had been published in 1976.

[14]*op. cit.,* Chapters 8,9,10 and 12.

Sobrino, writing more briefly in a single chapter of his book,[15] has a different approach. He expresses his commitment to check the christological formulae by what we know of the historical Jesus, because it is a theological responsibility, and to check our perceptions of the historical Jesus by the christological formulations, because it is an ecclesial responsibility. Following this route, he finds the perennial generic truth of the classic formulation unhelpful to Christian understanding unless mediated historically in the various cultural, social and philosophical settings. In particular, in terms of the human questions that we must ask today he finds the classic formulations lacking concreteness, historicity and relationality. [16] He concludes that these lacking elements cannot be extrapolated from the classic formulae themselves but must be built up alongside of them, which he proceeds to do.[17]

Besides the notable contributions of these two authors there is a strong though only implicit Christology in the ecclesiology of Ignacio Ellacuria.[18] What he implies with the title, *Freedom made Flesh*, and the development of thought in his book, is an approach that moves from the experience of liberation in Christ on the part of the community of believers, to an appreciation of Jesus as the liberator, and from there to a reflection on the human freedom of Jesus himself and the realization that it is the human embodiment of the divine

---

[15]*op. cit.*, Chapter 10.

[16]*ibid.* pp.328-332.

[17]*ibid.*pp.332-342.

[18]*op. cit.*

freedom.[19] Ellacuria has not elaborated this into an explicit Christology so far.[20]

It is not the intent of this book to dispute either the method or the conclusions of any of these authors. On the contrary, anything contained in the second part of this book is very heavily indebted to them and is intended to offer complementary insights, imagery and approach. Indeed it is to be hoped that this volume may contribute in some measure towards bridging the gap between the liberation theologians of the third world and the northern hemisphere theologians who are on the whole still unacquainted with them or hostile to them or both.

The return to the sources on the part of the liberation theologians has been two-pronged. It is not only a return to more careful reading of the accounts of the historical Jesus in their own context, but it is also a return to the lived experience of the community in the present as a source for theological reflection in the context of the entire history of the Christian community. The first part of this, the return to more careful study of the historical Jesus, none have disputed, at least in principle. The latter part has been bitterly disputed because the emphasis, sometimes the exclusive emphasis, has been on the experience of the poor and the oppressed. This has prompted critics to point out that the oppressed and poor are not demonstrably more virtuous or more docile to the gospel than others, while they are, however, demonstrably less

[19]*ibid.*, Chapters 2 and 3.

[20]He disclaims the intention, *ibid.*, *p.* 27.

learned and therefore less apt in assimilation of data and analysis of issues. Moreover, it is claimed, a bias in favor of the poor is as much a bias (and therefore as untrue to the gospel) as a bias in favor of the learned or the rich. Perhaps we need a further clarification of what it is in the contemporary experience of Christians that constitutes a source for theological reflection in general and for Christology in particular.

The source of Christology is, in the first place, Christian experience in three dimensions: the experience of conversion; the experience of community; and the experience of death, conflict and peace. In the second place, the source for Christology is the record of these experiences, especially as testified by those who knew the historical Jesus and those who participated in the first ecstatic experiences of the presence of the risen Christ. In the third place, not so much a source but rather a common language and a set of guidelines are offered by the official formulations crystallized out of the fluid tradition by a complex discernment and reflection process of the institutional church.

Central to the process of Christology from the beginning has been the experience of conversion in Christ and reflection upon the cause, nature and effect of such conversion. This seems to be the thrust of the Ascension and Pentecost stories; the witnesses will have something to say to the world about the difference that Jesus makes and about who Jesus is when the "power from on high" will have transformed their own experience and response by clarity of vision and courage of conviction. It is, of course, possible to study the early testimonies in order to arrive at a descriptive account of what the conversion of the early witnesses really was in terms of altered consciousness and behavior. But there is no way to distill this into a culture-free or culturally neutral definition to be applied directly in all situations. What the interpretation of those early testimonies really depends upon is the continuing participation in the same community event by successive generations of Christians all experiencing the Christian conversion in their own cultural and socio-economic context.

It is clear that strong voices are being raised today to testify to the nature and circumstances of that conversion as they have experienced it. They come from charismatic communities proclaiming a rebirth of trust in God, sense of intimate presence of God and inner rootedness and serenity. They come also from communities engaged in social action, proclaiming a rebirth of courage, vision and hope, and of a new-found prophetic consciousness of the dimensions of sin in the structures of our society. These two movements are not incompatible with each other but rather complementary, and it is precisely when they are seen as complementary that they offer the foundation for a contemporary Christology that is theoretically and practically coherent.

The experience of conversion is known most intimately in one's own life by introspection. It is known in the lives of others by inference from their behavior and by empathy with the accounts they give of themselves. However, there is also an experience of conversion which is shared. It is the conversion of structures which we call community. In the contemporary Christian experience community has become a dominant element among those who claim to be newly and more deeply converted, and this finds a ready counterpart in the testimonies of the apostolic period that we find in the Acts of the

Apostles and the letters of Paul. In both cases it is described as a discovery, a gift and a foretaste of heaven. The transformation of social structures governing the relationships among those who have undergone a personal, adult conversion is recognized as the process of redemption, reversing the structures established by sin. The transformation of structures into true community is recognized as first fruits of the redemption.

This contemporary awareness of and focus on community is common to the charismatic groups and the social action groups and to many other clusters of Christians who would not consider themselves as belonging to either of these two types. The widespread movement calling itself "basic Christian communities" combines many characteristics of both types. Among them there is a tacit understanding, sometimes explicitly voiced, that Jesus is savior because he liberates from the futility of sin and alienation which is known in the social structures of selfishness, reckless competition and oppression. He liberates into the freedom of communion with God, the other dimension of which is non-exclusive community with fellow human beings. Jesus is known as divine because this liberation out of futility and isolation is the work of God recreating out of the shambles of a sinful history, and because this liberation is self-validating both at the deepest levels of human experience and at all reaches of complexity in human organization. We do not know the divine in itself but we can recognize its ordering, focussing, harmonizing power in our lives.

To speak of Christian experience as the source of Christology is, of course, to include the experiences of death, conflict and peace. In every human situation in history, people must confront death, deal with conflict and find peace. The circumstances and perceptions of death and conflict vary, as do the definitions of peace, but the quest always has those common elements and to know Jesus as savior, recognizing in him the power of the divine presence, is to know him in relation to that quest for peace in face of death and conflict. Again, this quest has both an intimate individual and a public social aspect. It is both a very private and a shared experience. It is concerned with human consciousness but also with social structures at all levels of complexity. The perception and the manner of the quest is conditioned by cultural, economic, social and political circumstances in which individuals and societies live, and it is out of this variety that Christians must reflect on their lives as followers of Jesus, asking and answering the question concerning the difference that Jesus makes and the way we are to understand his identity.

This then, in the first place, is the source for a Christology. But a Christology does not spring up anew in each age from nowhere. We begin with expectations and formulae of worship and belief that are ages old and are given in the context of a living tradition of life-styles and interaction which is ages old. We share in a process that has continued for a long time and has established certain foundations and ground rules. Even if we do not intend it, our reflections arise not out of our present experience in isolation but out of our present experience as we perceive and interpret it in the light of our traditions as we have appropriated them. Inescapably, therefore, a second source of our Christology, intertwined with the first, is the record of Christian experience from the beginning, testified by each generation and interpreted cumulatively through the ages in Scripture, liturgy, iconography, legend, devotional practices and so forth.

Our own experience arises within this tradition and, as it becomes more personal, more reflective, more intense, it differentiates itself from what has been handed on out of the experiences of others, and it enters into continuing dialogue with what has been handed on from others. In a normal development of Christian life there is, so to speak, a "take-off point" of theological adulthood at which uncritical assimilation of verbal and ritual repetition yields to theological reflection which takes one's own experience seriously. There may, of course, be an intervening adolescence in which only one's own experience is taken seriously as though it contained all knowledge and sustained all wisdom. But, like any adolescence, this is a transition to the integration of what we know from our own experience with what we know from the experience and cumulative wisdom of others.

In a heavily doctrinal church tradition like the Catholic this raises special questions concerning the role in this process which is played by dogmatic definitions carrying the authority of the teaching office of the institutional church. They have often been regarded as the end of the process, as though after that the experience of succeeding generations could play no role other than simple confirmation of the formula. Against this, contemporary believers have protested that formulations such as the Christological explanations of Chalcedon are simply not adequate to play such a role. Early in his career, Karl Rahner expressed this by claiming that Chalcedon must be seen not as the end of Christological reflection but as the beginning.[21] Considering the matter now, in the light of the

[21]"Current Questions in Christology," *Theological Studies*, vol. 1 (Baltimore: Helicon, 1961) pp. 149-200.

questions that have been raised in our times, especially by the liberation theologians, one must go further and say that Chalcedon is not a beginning either, but it is a marker along the way which serves as one, though not the only, criterion of orthodoxy, Scripture and liturgy being more important and more comprehensive but also more diffuse and elusive criteria of orthodoxy.

4

History and Interpretation

The Promised Reign of God

Crucial in the task of Christology is the way we approach the person of Jesus. Modern scholarly reflection has made the distinction between the Jesus of history and the Christ of faith.[1] This was, clearly, a necessary distinction: there are on the one hand the historical testimonies concerning Jesus and on the other hand the proclamations of faith, naming him Christ and Lord, Word of God and Savior. There is on the one

[1]The issue is explained very clearly by Joseph Bourke, "The Historical Jesus and the Kerygmatic Christ," *Who is Jesus of Nazareth?*, ed. E. Schillebeeckx and B. Willems (N.Y.: Paulist, 1965), pp. 27-46; and Avery Dulles, *Myth, Biblical Revelation and Christ* (Washington: Corpus Books, 1968).

hand the temporarily and spatially limited life-span of an individual who lived long ago in another culture. But there is on the other hand the all-embracing claim of the Resurrection, a breakthrough into a radically different and universally pervasive presence and power.

This raises, in the first place, the question concerning the relationship between the two — the relationship between the historical individual, Jesus, and the pervasive presence and power experienced by Christians and identified by them as the Risen Christ. This also means that the question concerns the relationship between what has been said and may be said of the historical Jesus, on the one hand, and what has been said and may be said of the risen Christ of Christian faith, on the other. This has provoked much discussion. Yet it is not the issue that is most urgent and important today.

The urgent questions today concern the proper reading of the testimonies concerning Jesus with specific reference to the kind of salvation they promise. They concern, therefore, the relationship between his teaching and the Jewish tradition from which he drew his language, symbolism and religious heritage. They concern the relationship also between the life-style, teaching and death of Jesus and the political situation of his people at that time. They concern in a special way his relationship with and his attitudes towards the various religious-political movements and stances of his Jewish contemporaries.

Scholarly efforts have been devoted to discovering as precisely as possible what was the stance of Jesus in these three contexts. However, what has become quite apparent is that such investigations are very much conditioned by the political, religious, cultural and philosophical presuppositions of those making the investigation. Our modern Western, post-Enlightenment assumption of the essentially private nature of religious faith and commitment seems to have obscured our perceptions of the Jewish expectations of salvation and of the political import of the teaching of Jesus in his own times.[2] Those reflections, therefore, which come from the Christian communities of the oppressed of our times have a particular value in redressing the balance. Out of the "basic Christian communities" among the poor and oppressed have come the attempts of the liberation theologians to approach the questions concerning the historical Jesus from a wider base of human experience.

Although it does not at first appear as a question related to this concern to reinstate the experience of the oppressed in theological reflection, the relation of the preaching and attitudes and expectations of Jesus to the traditions of his Hebrew heritage is crucial. Jesus did not claim to found a new religion, but to uncover anew the truth of the Hebrew tradition and to bring it to maturity. As we look back to the testimonies concerning the Jesus of history, there are some aspects of this uncovering that are beyond dispute. For him there is no profane realm, because the relationship with the Creator-Father does not consist of ritual religious activities but of the totality of life. For him there is also no possibility of separating the intimate communion with the Father from all-inclusive fostering care of fellow human beings.

It is clear, and the Gospels underscore it often enough, that the preaching and healing ministry of Jesus is rooted in his profound compassion for the confusion and disorientation of

---

[2]*Cf.* John Howard Yoder, *The Politics of Jesus* (Grand Rapids: Eerdmans, 1972).

his fellow countrymen, and most especially the poor and unlearned, who suffer not only the indignities and hardships of the Roman occupation, but also and more poignantly a certain alienation from God's promised saving reign among them. This concern with the Reign of God appears in the Gospels as the all-consuming passion of the historical Jesus, and therefore the content and manner of that Reign as Jesus understood it seems to be the most important information we need to seek about the Jesus of history.

We know a good deal about the Jewish understanding of the Reign of God at the time of Jesus, and can safely infer more.[3] The argument among scholars is not so much concerned with the accepted Jewish understanding of the Reign of God as with the question about the modification in that understanding which Jesus may or may not have made.[4] The Hebrew understanding is related to the stories of creation and sin and the struggle in history that results from the cumulative consequences of evil deeds. By the very fact of creation, God is the Master of the Universe, the Lord of History, but the freedom of the human person is an invitation to acknowledge that Lordship, giving it reality in a new way.

The story of the Garden and the eating of the forbidden fruit is a story of the human seizure of what is at the center of creation and holds creation together in harmony — a harmony that can only be maintained by God. The story of the Fall with its stark sequels of fratricide and treacheries and bullying, suggests that the peaceful community of human

---

[3]See Rudolf Schnackenburg, *God's Rule and Kingdom* (N.Y.: Herder, 1963)

[4]*Cf.* Helmut Riedlinger, "The Universal Kingship of Christ," in *Who is Jesus of Nazareth?* pp. 27-46; Oliver Rousseau, "The Idea of the Kingship of Christ," *ibid.*, pp.129-143; and especially Jon Sobrino, *op. cit.*, Chapter 3.

persons is only possible in the unqualified acknowledgement of the Lordship of God. The entire biblical history of Israel and the comments thereon in the Law and the Prophets and the Writings are concerned with the hope and possibility of salvation from this state of confusion and disorientation.

This is the context of the Covenant that makes Israel God's people, espousing them to him by the sharing of God's own wisdom in the Law. This is the context also of the retrospective reflection on the problem of the kings in the history of the people. Thus, in I Samuel 8, the conversation there represented between God and Samuel offers a sobering contrast between the way God rules and the way earthly governments can be expected to rule, for God's Reign is without self-interest. Yet there is acknowledgement also of the need for order and government in a sinful history, and a consequent ambivalence about the role of governments that are based on self-interest and self-aggrandizement and are therefore often far from perfect in achieving justice and harmony in society. And this ambivalence runs through the whole biblical history of Israel and forms part of the heritage of Jesus and his contemporaries.

Yet also part of that heritage is the never forgotten hope of a more radical deliverance by the establishment of God's own Reign, as that is intended in the very plan of creation and renewed in a special way within sinful history by the great Covenant of God with his people. That hope in turn gives rise to the expectation of a more worthy vice-regent to stand as human and historical representative of God in the ordering of a just and holy society in peace and harmony and in the joy of a full communion with God. Although the expectation of Messiah, the anointed or elect, has never been as clear-cut and explicitly precise in the traditions of Israel as Christians have commonly supposed, there is no doubt that there was the expectation of human mediation of God's reign of justice and peace. There is also no doubt that that Reign of justice and peace, restoring the proper order of the rightful and saving Lordship of God was understood as this-worldly, giving focus to history in hope and fidelity.[5]

The crucial question for Christians, then, is whether Jesus modified this expectation only by the immediacy and unconditional character of his vision of the coming Reign of God, or also by envisaging it as other-worldly, purely private and spiritual, separating the religious realm from the workings of the larger structures of society by which people's lives and possibilities are so largely shaped. In the post-Enlightenment era, largely by reaction to the obvious inconsistencies of "Christendom," there has been a prevailing assumption, at least in Western Christian thought, that the proper sphere of religious faith is in the private aspects of individual lives and in the strictly religious, ecclesiastical activities of communities of believers. This seems to have carried over into the further assumption that Jesus must have been likewise concerned with this private religious sphere. As a result, the questions which we have commonly asked in studying the New Testament testimonies concerning the preaching and intent of Jesus, were already conditioned to expect very private answers.

[5]For the necessarily political content of the Hebrew understanding of the Lordship of Yahweh, *cf.* J.P.M. Walsh, "Lordship of Yahweh, Lordship of Jesus," in *Above Every Name.*, pp. 35-65.

A re-reading of the evidence with awareness of the bias we have been superimposing on it from our modern conscious-ness, suggests a much broader, more concretely earthy con-tents to the Reign of God as understood by Jesus. His exhortations, for instance, are constantly concerned with the relationships among persons. The parables are drawn from everyday life and from the social structures of the time. The way to welcome the Reign of God is by rather radical ways of behavior, challenging the prevailing injustices in non-violent ways, and overcoming traditional hostilities and fears by bold community-building gestures of reconciliation by transcend-ing the modes in which the problems are being perpetuated. Moreover, the actual patterns of interaction of the early post-Resurrection communities express an interpretation of the teachings of Jesus which evidently understands the Reign of God as very much concerned with the concrete structures of human society.

This raises important questions as to why there is so little in the Gospels that testifies to direct criticism by Jesus of the structures of the political power of the Roman occupation, with its oppression, injustices and cruelties. Again, we tend too quickly to read this silence with the bias of our own perception of political possibilities, forgetting that in the absence of a democratic form of government and without the possibility of invoking international sanctions to support a protest, the choices at the time of Jesus were very different from the choices that we have. Practically speaking, the choice lay apparently between the violence of a military uprising (which the Romans always feared, and many Jews dreamed of and planned) and the inactivity of submission to a political situation accepted as inevitable (which seems to have been the more common choice). Yet the Gospels clearly record that Jesus rejected both military rebellion and passive acceptance of the status quo as inevitable. The first was the stance of the Zealots and the *sicarii*, which Jesus certainly refused to entertain,[6] and the second was the position of both the Pharisaic and the Sadducean parties, with whom Jesus had firm, if sometimes subtle, differences in his approach to social issues.[7]

It would seem that Jesus saw another option which emerged from a far more radical analysis of the injustices and sinfulness of the situation. He appears to have been far less concerned with what the Romans did to Jews than with what Jews did or failed to do, individually and together, as God's people. But this should not immediately be seen as a non-political stand. It might be seen rather as directly in line with the history and expectations of Israel. Escape from Egypt, in the classic foundation story of the people, did not mean escape from injustice and oppression, for they soon found, even in their desert wanderings how easily they could fall into oppressing and even enslaving one another, and how much they needed the wisdom and restraint of the Law. Constantly the biblical writers play variations on the theme that when Israel does justly and compassionately among its own people, respecting God's Law, it will have peace with other nations and will enjoy prosperity, but when it does unjustly, setting aside God's Law, it will suffer conquests, occupations, exiles and heavy burdens of oppression.

---

[6]*Cf.* Oscar Cullmann, *Jesus and the Revolutionaries* (N.Y.: Harper & Row, 1970); and Martin Hengel, *Was Jesus a Revolutionist?* (Philadelphia: Fortress, 1971).

[7]*Cf.* Richard J. Cassidy, *op. cit.*

If this was simply the concern of Jesus, to evoke a return to God's reign among his own people, in the conviction that to do justly and compassionately according to God's Law is the principle for the restructuring of all human society, then the most direct approach would be a "grass-roots" approach. Moreover, it would require a strategy of non-violence, but of non-violent resistance to evil in a manner that could be truly revolutionary in the restructuring of human society,[8] and as such essentially political and essentially religious at the same time.[9]

This much has in fact been uncovered by contemporary scholarship, though not without much debate. However, something ought to be said about the relationship between faith and criticism. Ever since Tertullian in the early third century, it has been claimed that, the Bible being the Church's book, it is the Church that has the right to interpret it. There is much to be said for this, for the meaning of the texts is far more than that of the original authors and certainly far more than can be elicited by scholarly inquiry. The testimonies to Jesus as Savior were selected and gathered into the canon of the New Testament as the outcome of a widely diffused process of discernment among the local communities of Christians (functioning largely as the "basic Christian communities" do today). We know of the redaction history of individual documents, that it was not a case of methodically sifting evidence to produce a reliable chronicle of events, but rather a case of discerning in the Spirit what texts best

[8]*Cf.* Yoder, *op. cit.* for an interesting approach to this.

[9]This is discussed further in Chapters 5 and 12.

expressed the truth of Jesus as recognized from the lived experience of the Christian life of the community.

History and interpretation take on a different aspect in a believer's Christology, because it is more than an archaeological expedition attempting to reconstitute a past event exactly as it was or could have been observed at the time. Rather it is an attempt to see the past event in the fulness of meaning which its impact on later history has been and still is unfolding. More particularly it is an approach to that meaning from within the continuing event, extended in the present participation in the life of the Risen Christ in the community. Questions of liberation, transformation of structures, evaluation of practical possibilities of peace, attitudes to class struggles, and so forth, which were not explicitly addressed at the time of Jesus or in the formation of the New Testament, can yet become integral questions of a Christology, because the concern is with the Risen Christ as a living and continuing reality in Christian history.

Our Christology is indeed always rooted and anchored in history — first and foremost the history of the individual life of Jesus, but then also, in a wider sense, the history of the impact of the Risen Christ as it continues up to and in the present.[10] This means that a believer's Christology may find the historical Jesus of scholarly investigation dessicated almost to the point of irrelevance, while the scholar may continue to find the believer's Christology distasteful and confusing. Moreover, the believer's Christology will tend to shape itself

---

[10]Thus E. Schillebeeckx proposes that a person is truly known in his capacity to make history. *Jesus* (N.Y.: Seabury, 1979)

in different ways according to the exigencies of Christian life as met by different communities. It will not confine itself to the models proposed in the New Testament nor to that of Chalcedon, though it will regard both with respect. It will not suppose that when one model appears as right and appropriate, others are therefore wrong and inappropriate. Whatever is truly a believer's Christology is marked by an awareness of the inadequacy and analogical character of all religious language, and is therefore at home with paradox and change. It is from this perspective that a believer's Christology approaches history and interpretation.

Part II
Proposal Towards A
Constructive Christology

5

The Preaching of Jesus and the

Reign of God

Two points about the preaching of Jesus are agreed: his teaching focussed on the hope and expectation and promise of God's reign among human persons, and that teaching had a clarity and confidence that did not come from book learning. The previous chapter has already discussed the relationship of Jesus' proclamation to the existing Jewish expectation of the Reign of God, to the social questions of his time and to the religious-social movements in Israel that also addressed those questions. It may, however, be helpful to consider how the preaching and healing ministry of Jesus could be expected to further the coming of the promised Reign that would bring salvation and redemption from the suffering of sin.

The teaching of Jesus as presented to us in the Gospels has, as it were, two dimensions. It is concerned with the human experience of, and attitude to, the transcendent God, and it is also concerned with the human experience of, and attitude to, fellow human beings. In the first of these, recent scholarship has constantly pointed out the prominence of the "Abba-experience" of Jesus in the portraits of him which the evangelists offer us.[1] As far as we can know, the intimacy of the way that Jesus himself perceived God was unique to Jesus and cannot be traced to what he learned from his culture and tradition. It emerges as the critical reflection on his own praxis.

It is surely a very important part of Christian theology to attempt to enter into that praxis by empathy, and the constant focus on the Kingdom of Heaven to be found in Matthew's Gospel, suggests a point of entry into such an attempt at empathy. The phrase that Matthew uses is clearly reminiscent of the inter-testamental scribal teaching which names the hope and concern of Israel as the "reign (or kingdom) of the heavens."[2] What we know of this inter-testamental scribal teaching is very helpful in understanding the way Jesus relates to the transcendent God.

In response to the questions of crushed and persecuted but faithful Jews, the scribes promised that the day of the great vindication would come by God's own reckoning and in God's own way, wonderfully, powerfully, fulfilling human dreams beyond all imagining. The language used was that of

---

[1] *Cf.* Joachim Jeremias, *New Testament Theology, vol. 1: The Proclamation of Jesus* (N.Y.: Scribner, 1971).

[2] *Cf.* "Basileia" by K. L., Schmidt, H. Kleinknecht, K. G. Kuhn and Gerhard von Rad, in *Dictionary of the New Testament*, Vol. 2., ed. Gerhard Kittel, (N.Y.: Harper & Row, 1958).

metaphor and was apocalyptic in style. In response to requests
for further clarification, the scribal tradition offered this per-
ceptive answer: "Live now as though God reigned and no-one
else had any power over you; fulfill the commandments of
God with that passionate commitment that seeks to read
between the lines, discerning that which cannot be prescribed
but which is the heart of the great covenant God makes with
his people; do this and you yourself shall, so to speak, see the
reign of God (the Kingdom of the Heavens) coming. You will
see it, as it were, from within."

This sublime teaching echoes, of course, the traditional mid-
rashic image that the first set of tablets of the Law—the ones
that Moses broke—were quite blank, because the essence of
the covenant of God with his people cannot be spelt out in
explicit and specific commands, but involves constant discernment possible only in the context of the loyalty of total
personal commitment and intimate presence. The New Testament reflects often on this with the concern of Jesus that it is
the "spirit" and not the "letter" of the Law that is significant,
and with the understanding that Jesus calls his followers
friends and not servants, and again with the theme of the
Spirit given to the followers so that they themselves may
discern and may understand.

In the light of this tradition and the Christian appropriation
of it, Jesus emerges as the one who, more than any other, in an
outstanding way, fulfilled the invitation to Israel to live now as
though God alone reigned and no-one else had any power to
punish or enforce. His attitude relativizes and diminishes, one
might say dwarfs, the power of those who can kill the body,
but cannot touch spirit or purpose or vision. Characteristics of
Jesus which the evangelists note again and again, and which

apparently struck people most forcefully, were his quiet confidence, his ready and immense compassion for any kind of suffering, the utter simplicity of his approach to life and people and theological or ethical problems, and his deep and spontaneous piety. He was never overawed by wealth, power or learning, nor was he reluctant or embarrassed to be associated with the disreputable. There was a certain childlike directness in the way he approached people.

All these things we can say with great assurance about the historical Jesus. Whether or not particular stories of encounters, miracles, conversations or sermons, are chronicles of actual events or constructs giving a broader interpretation of the meaning and impact of Jesus, the testimonies of the Gospels and the life-style of those who subsequently lived as his followers, give eloquent witness to these as the characteristics that people most clearly saw and most eagerly admired in Jesus. But all these characteristics also speak very clearly of a life lived as though God now reigned and none else had power. The Gospels suggest that this focus in life came to Jesus out of his tradition and out of his personal prayer. The tradition of Israel as he appropriated it appears to have been according to the spirituality of the *anawim*, the "poor in spirit" or simple people who placed all their trust in God. The stance to which he came out of his personal prayer seems to have led him by way of the preaching of the Baptist to a prophetic outlook that took a very critical look at the social structures and injustices by which people were crushed.

What is typical of Jesus is the easy combination of the two perspectives—that of total trust in God and that of radical criticism of what caused human suffering. The preaching of the Baptist as we know it was grim, a prophecy of doom, calling for repentance because Israel was once more on the threshold of disaster. The preaching of Jesus calls for repentance also and, as has been pointed out frequently in recent scholarship, was fully aware that the practical fate of Israel, God's witness people, hung in the balance between disaster and the Reign of God coming.[3] Yet the preaching of Jesus calls for repentance because God is ever-loving, ever-forgiving. The change in emphasis and motivation is striking. It is the dominant theme in the parables of Jesus and it is the constant pattern of his relationships with individuals.

The Gospels give us a number of glimpses into the vision and imagination of Jesus and into the kinds of observations and experiences that seem to have shaped his image of God and of God's dealings with creation.[4] They are observations and experiences of nature and of people which the traditions of Israel and its psalmody and wisdom had expressed before, but they appear in the sayings of Jesus with personal intimacy and warmth and spontaneity. The observations of the breathtaking beauty of the short-lived wild flowers, of the lovable simplicity and frailty of the despised ubiquitous sparrows picking a modest living out of the refuse, of the grandeur of the skies over the sea of Galilee eloquent with promise or threat to fishermen and herdsmen and farmers—all these things speak of times of quiet contemplation of the world. And all these things are easily, spontaneously linked in the words of Jesus (and therefore, we know, in his own thought and outlook)

---

[3]See a succinct summary of this in Schillebeeckx, *Jesus* (N.Y.: Seabury, 1979), pp. 115-178.

[4]This is considered in some detail in Brian McDermott, "Power and Parable in Ministry," in *Above Every Name*, ed. Thomas E. Clarke (N.Y.: Paulist, 1980), pp. 83-104.

with the over-arching, intimately involved, compassionate providence of God.

There is a tenderness and immediacy in these reflections which appears to be in the first place the warm immediacy of Jesus' own presence to the living things of creation, and in the second place his recognition in his own attitudes of the warm immediacy of the Creator's presence which he, Jesus, reflects and expresses in his own being. It may be this sense of spontaneous and comfortable identification which leads to the gentle humor and delicate pathos of imaging God as the poor woman who scrambles after the coin that rolls away on the mud floor in her dark little house, for God is most anxious to rescue any bit of his precious creation that may be rolling way from him in the obscurity of a sinful history. Even better is the example that images God as a rascally shepherd (for they did not have a good reputation) who is not about to lose a single valuable sheep, and will take risks with the herd to recapture a stray animal. But most daring and at the same time the simplest of all, is the imaging of God as a father who cannot afford to lose a son, because the son is part of himself, because he feels that his own destiny is bound up with his son's, and because the straying of his son is his own suffering and loss.

Out of the contemplation and personal prayer of Jesus, schooled in the prayer traditions of Israel, comes this all-pervading sense that the Creator-God who "fathers" all creatures and has "fathered" him, Jesus, is benignly and passionately present as the head of the household of his creation—though as one whose dedication to his family is much abused, forgotten and misrepresented. It is clear that as Jesus images God as the father of the family of creation, so he also images himself as son and is at ease in that role to the point that the familiar designation, "Abba," impressed but apparently did not surprise his friends.

How Jesus experiences the relationship between attitudes to God and attitudes to fellow human beings is expressed in many ways, but perhaps never more poignantly than in the story of the elder son, the elder brother of the boy gone astray. It is family piety that holds the two aspects together—the affectionate, grateful love of God and the caring concern for people. As the father is intimately involved in the fate of his son and suffers intensely the alienation of his wilfulness, so the elder brother, if he is truly identified with the father, suffers with keenest empathy the alienation of the younger brother. The ultimate tragedy in human affairs is not that there is a history of sin and alienation, but that redemptive compassion and true empathy have died out in the experience of those who claim to live in the father's house and to be about the father's business.

Jesus, so the evangelists tell us, leaves the relative comfort and security of a craftman's life in Nazareth out of compassion for the alienated, for those officially designated sinners or ignorant of the Law of God, for those apparently too poor or insignificant to be taken into account in the expectation of God's glorious Reign. The preaching appears to have dealt with the familiar category of the reign of God—the category that expressed the existing hope of Israel. But the Reign of God as Jesus proclaims it is not the triumphant march of the great monarch coming to claim tribute and announcing his advent while yet a long way off—perhaps thousands of years in the future. Rather it is the Reign of God coming as Jesus has understood it by living as though God now reigned and none else had any power in the world. Jesus has indeed lived like that, and has seen the Reign of God coming from within the Kingdom to which his own participation has admitted him. What he has found and what he shares with the poor and the abandoned is that it is the rule of a compassionate, concerned father in his own family, not intent upon judgement and condemnation but intent upon drawing the family together again in peace and joy under his roof.

It is clear that there is supposed to be a connection between the preaching of Jesus and the coming of the Reign of God. Indeed, it seems that in the early part of the ministry of Jesus there is a great optimism in his way of proclaiming the compassionate yearning of God for the reconciliation and peace of his human creation. He seems, at this stage, to see his task as that of encouraging his listeners to take simple but quite radical steps of trust, reciprocal forgiveness, and solidarity in the acknowledgement of human dignity. In the preaching of Jesus the Reign of God is the gift of God, but it is a gift already offered, waiting only to be welcomed and received in the human response of trust and reconciliation which is the inevitable condition of the Reign of God among human persons. Jesus seems to see the first steps as inexpressibly simple and, in view of the compassionate welcome of God, as not difficult to take.

As the evangelists present Jesus, he in his own person, his life-style, his ways of relating to people, his actions and his words, was a constant invitation to trust God and make the leap of faith involved in welcoming the Reign of God in one's life and community. The impact of his presence on people was healing, reconciling, forgiving in spiritual, psychological, social and physical ways. His preaching ministry in itself was already redemptive, anticipating the Reign of God which he proclaimed.

If we ask more particularly how it was that the presence and ministry of Jesus mediated redemption to those whom he met and influenced, the Gospels answer us that he overcame blindness, deafness and hardness of heart in people, that he encouraged them out of their paralysis, loved them out of their panic and confusion, released them from crippling physical and psychological burdens, brought them back to life. But the Gospels also tell us that the principal concern of Jesus was to refocus and re-educate their imagination. Legalism, superstition, lack of basic self worth and the pervasive, crippling fear of a generally oppressed consciousness, seem to have cramped and withered their power to image God or their own future or the possibilities of their own present society. And this paralysis of imagination was evidently projected onto God as the harsh judge and taskmaster, as the distant one who no longer granted the gift of prophecy or the present revelation of his wisdom and purpose in the world.

Perhaps it is precisely in those sayings of Jesus that we consider "hard sayings," those which call for radical responses of forgiveness, non-retaliation of injuries, far-reaching generosity in the sharing of goods, basic renunciations of personal satisfactions, or uncompromising detachment, that Jesus is most compassionate. He attempts to share his own clear-eyed vision of the Reign of God coming by trying to coax others into the experience out of which his own vision comes—the experience of truly living now as though God reigned and there were no other consequences to fear. The tragedy of the life of Jesus begins with the realization that both then and now we are all too trapped, too entrammelled in the structures of sin to dare to leap as far as he invites us. But the compassion of Jesus grows to boundless proportions in that he continues his healing and rebuilding ministry where he can and follows us into the trap.

6

The Dynamics of Tragedy in the

Death of Jesus

Even to strangers and outsiders to the Christian faith, Jesus is an heroic figure because of the manner of his death and the dedication of his life which led to that death. Strangely enough, outsiders sometimes appear to appreciate the tragedy of the death of Jesus more than Christians. Our religious language and imagery has made the cross a symbol of the sacred, of salvation, of the power of God, and we are too easily able to forget that behind the liturgical symbol lies a secular reality that is devastating in its meaning and its wider implications. The understanding that the death of Jesus by crucifixion is salvific is such a total reversal of our ordinary human wisdom that it requires a far greater conversion of vision and judgement than is usually acknowledged in the conversation of Christians.

The tragedy of Jesus begins, of course, long before his arrest, trial and execution. It begins when his listeners, at first eager enough, balk at the simple totality of the leap of faith which his teaching on the Reign of God demands. It does not seem to be the case that he was misunderstood, but rather that he was understood too clearly. The implications of his teaching were revolutionary in a more radical sense than even the courageous revolutionaries of his time were prepared to follow. Much in the gospel accounts of the public ministry of Jesus suggests that he could have raised an improvised army of thousands at several points in his brief career, and that many of his followers hoped that he would do so.

It would seem that the aim of Jesus was too radical for his followers because it did not allow an easy division of the world into the forces of good and evil. It did not enable faithful Jews to identify the power of evil with the foreign domination of the Romans and their immediate collaborators. It did not allow them to identify oppression with the outsiders. Therefore it did not allow them to draw up battle lines and fight for freedom and God's Reign. In fact, it did not allow them to project the force and power of sin outside themselves into some exterior population, or structure.

This much has usually been freely acknowledged by Christians. However, it does not mean that the interest of Jesus was non-political and purely religious. Indeed in the Jewish attitudes and thought and teaching of his time, the idea that the political was not a matter of religious interest would have been a rather absurd idea. The interest of Jesus was surely all-embracing, because his concern was with the welcoming of

God's own rule in human society in fidelity to the Jewish hope and the promises made to Israel. What made the teaching of Jesus different and apparently so hard to accept then as now, was that it required a critical reassessment of the structures and values and attitudes of human society as his listeners and followers shared in it. It required an acknowledgement of the inauthenticity, the selfishness and the destructive character of one's own mode of articulation into the society.

What the listeners apparently discerned quite correctly was that this was no invitation to repentance that simply called for an acknowledgement of sinfulness and helplessness in the situation while waiting for the salvation of God to come somehow from outside the situation and outside of human freedom. Jesus proclaimed the presence of the Reign of God now, if only they would accept it. In other words he proclaimed that the grace or gift of God was not being promised for the future and withheld in the present but was present empowerment for a totally different kind of life and society. If the empowerment of God is already there, it leaves his listeners with the burden of response, the burden of risk in a radical change of lifestyle and relationships and expectations.

The keynote of all this, as his listeners correctly saw, is vulnerability. To live now as though God alone reigned in human affairs and no sanctions, reprisals or injustices were to be feared, is by all ordinary standards plain foolishness while in fact God does not really reign in human affairs. It is self-interest and greed for wealth and lust for power over others and a desperate unslakable thirst for recognition and status which rule the affairs of human society for the most part now as then. Those of us who hold relatively privileged positions in society do not always advert to this because there is an established law and order in society which regulates how much bullying and grabbing can be tolerated and what is beyond the acceptable limit. This law and order in any society is always so arranged as to give a certain stability by maintaining the existing patterns of privilege. It is the poor and the oppressed, the marginated and the despised, who can more readily see that the basic pattern of human relations is not concern for the common good but rampant competitive self-interest.

Jesus seems to have preached primarily to the poor and unlearned, to those who were despised as sinners and those who were in many ways oppressed. He preached, therefore, to those who would most readily recognize what he meant in his radical criticism of the pattern of human relationships and structures of society. He preached to those who, in a sense, had the least to lose because their plight was most desperate. His preaching was a process of consciousness-raising. Jesus by his own life-style and attitudes, by his relationships with them and his strengthening, healing, affirming effect on them, was constantly giving them a sense of their own worth in God's eyes, and of the empowering presence of God among them. Jesus preached a grass-roots non-violent revolution. He offered them, in God's name, the possibility of total transformation of their lives and circumstances from fear to a sense of security in face of anything that might happen, and from suspicion and struggle for self-preservation to community concern under the ever-present providence of God.

Yet even for the poorest and most abandoned, this must still have looked like an insane degree of personal vulnerability. In a world of desperately competitive self-interest, to care for others, to practice non-violence, to seek neither wealth nor status nor power, is certainly to leave the door wide open for others to take advantage, push the non-competitor out of the way, and kick down and crush the non-violent (the non-retaliator), if not actually to launch a harsh persecution. Jesus invited his listeners and followers to make that same radical act of trust and surrender to God's way and rule which he himself had made, and to do it as a people discovering thereby a transformation of all the structures of society from the grass-roots upwards.

The tragedy of Jesus begins with the realization that his preaching should indeed have been very dangerous to established and oppressive interests. It was so perceived by the Romans and by their Jewish collaborators in the oppression of the people. He was persecuted and eventually arrested and tried and executed because he constituted such a great danger to the established oppressive order of society. It should have been every bit as dangerous as they thought it was, but it turned out that his preaching (at least immediately) was not dangerous at all because the people, then as now, did not really respond. None would take the risk of moving out into that kind of vulnerability without the guarantee of a bullying power, a law with extrinsic sanctions, to enforce an equal commitment from all. But this is a contradiction in terms. Jesus was speaking of, and envisaging, that law of God which is written in hearts and has no sanction other than its own intrinsic wisdom, its own intrinsic goodness and self-validating quality of redemption from suffering and sin.

The gospels imply that the polarization of forces against Jesus was some mixture of anger and fear from those whose unjust positions in society would be threatened by a popular response to his preaching (because all oppression rests on the fear and disorganization of the oppressed) with a rising wave of disillusionment on the part of those who at first were enthusiastic followers but later found this message so radical as to be simply insane. The impetus that took Jesus to his death was completely coherent on his side and followed the common sense logic of the world on the part of his persecutors. The kind of conversion to the coming and imminent Reign of God which he envisaged might look harmless enough in the beginning, but if it were really carried through it would cause a chain reaction that would shake human history from its very foundations, making a new heaven and a new earth in which the former patterns of privilege and power and wealth would make no sense at all.

And so Jesus went to his early and terrible death, disgraced, defeated, ridiculed and tortured. Yet the decision was not as simple as it tends to look to Christians in retrospect. Concerning the death of Jesus there are several questions that have to be asked and answered. First there is the question as to who killed him and why. Secondly there is the question as to why he walked into the trap with his eyes open and other options within his choice, as the evangelists testify. Thirdly there is the question as to why God could permit it and why in retrospect we should make the quite extraordinary claim that this death of Jesus is redemptive for the human race.

As to who killed Jesus and why, there appears to be little remaining dispute, though the findings are being incorporated into our contemporary Christologies only with some reluctance. Jesus died by a Roman execution on a charge of being a pretender to the Davidic throne and therefore a threat to the Roman occupation, a charge on which others before him had also been executed.[1] The charge was evidently levelled against him because he had such power to draw crowds and inspire them with their consciousness of being God's people, and because he had a reputation as a wonderworker and a fearless man, which seemed to give people new courage and hope. Perhaps most of all, he was accused as a pretender to the throne because he spoke with authority in the name of God, and exerted a spiritual leadership that was not within the recognized patterns of authority known to the Romans as within the safe and agreed role descriptions of the collaborators with the occupation forces.

Whether and what charges were also levelled against Jesus in the context of Jewish law seems to be a matter of much more dispute but it also seems to be more or less irrelevant. He was not executed by Jews and he was therefore not executed on charges having to do with Jewish law. The evangelists clearly intend to implicate the leaders, and especially the highpriestly family and party, in the betrayal of Jesus to the Romans. However, it is established fact that these high priestly functionaries were appointed by the Romans as safe and known collaborators who would do what was necessary to preserve their own positions, and would not be too scrupulous about it. Therefore, any accusations that the leaders of the Jews were to blame for the death of Jesus have to be placed in the context in which the leaders mentioned were such by Roman appointment and were acting accordingly in subordinate positions of the Roman occupation. If the Jewish crowds

---

[1] For a summary of what is known about the trial of Jesus, cf. Gerald Sloyan, *Jesus on Trial* (Philadelphia: Fortress, 1973); and Richard Cassidy, *op. cit*, Chapters 5 and 6.

were implicated as the passion narratives have them depicted, it would be rather in terms of not staging a tumultuous uprising in protest against the condemnation of Jesus—an uprising which would in any case have been counter to the preaching of Jesus.

It is in the context of a Roman arrest and a political execution for high treason (as we might formulate it), that the question must be asked as to why Jesus walked into the trap. The Gospels maintain that Jesus had other options even to the end—to keep a low profile and avoid Jerusalem at the time of the Passover feast, to retire to the country beyond the Jordan, perhaps to preach a quiet message of trust in God in the villages. However, to preach trust in God in the context of Jewish history necessarily suggested to people's imaginations a war of national liberation, given the folklore of the heroic past, the Exodus, the victories of David, and many other valiant leaders, most recently the evocative legends of the Maccabeans.

The option of returning to a quiet preaching and healing ministry once the sharp polarization against him had taken place, must have seemed to Jesus in some way a betrayal of his mission as he had come to understand it. That the discernment of what to do was difficult for him is attested by the evangelists in the stories of the withdrawals from the city for quiet and reflection, and is dramatized especially in the vivid visual story of the agony in the garden. It is probably also adumbrated by the stylized stories of the temptations in the desert in the beginning of the public ministry. In this matter of the reasons Jesus may have had for continuing his public presence in Jerusalem at a time when he knew he would be arrested, perhaps more than in any other matter related to the life and actions of Jesus, it is out of the praxis of their own lives as his followers that Christians must attempt to understand his mind. Indeed, this seems to have been largely what the evangelists themselves did, and Christian writers and preachers have done ever since.

Because this is so much a matter of reflection on one's own Christian praxis, the more academic theology of later ages has tended to focus attention almost exclusively on the obedience of Jesus to the Father, as though some message had been communicated to him directly that he should fulfill the prophecies and make amendments for sin by suffering this terrible death of the Roman scourging and crucifixion. The evangelists do indeed emphasize that the death of Jesus was in the final analysis obedience to the Father, but nothing suggests that that obedience was simply the execution of an explicit command. Far rather, the emphasis points to a process of laborious discernment of what were the possibilities within the situation—the possibilities of furthering the human welcome to the Reign of God. The account of the agony in the garden does not suggest that Jesus was anxious to end his career in this way, but rather that he comes to the decision by the elimination of other possibilities.

Again, because this matter is so much one of discerning out of the experience of one's own discipleship, a number of voices have been raised out of contemporary Third World experiences, suggesting a quite different approach.[2] They see Jesus as the typical, perhaps prototypical, liberator of the oppressed,

---

[2]*E.g.* Nolan, *op. cit.*, Chapters 14-16 offers a grim and quite new perspective on the logic that brought Jesus to his early death.

who becomes the target of the pent-up violence and fear of the oppressor. They see his decision as one that he has made bit by bit along the way in championing the oppressed, until he is a hunted man with no further choice except to survive for some time as a fugitive whose activities are strictly circumscribed, or to come out into the open with some last bold statements and suffer death forthwith. Clearly, this is a reading of the story of the polarization, the persecution, the arrest and trial and death, which fills in all the unknown details from the experience of Third World champions of liberation in our own time. It is based on the claim that the situation in which Jesus lived and died was far more closely akin to that of Third World peoples of our day than to that of the privileged classes of wealthy nations to which theologians more usually belong.[3]

Whichever way of filling in the unknown details may be the more probable, the fact remains that the discernment of the possibilities left to him brought Jesus to a deeper and deeper identification and solidarity with the most oppressed and most despised and outcast. Inasmuch as it did this, his path of discernment at the end of his life was fully in continuity with the focus of his preaching and ministry, for the key note in all of it was clearly that of compassion in the fullest sense of that word. Jesus enters progressively into the dilemma of the human situation and into the greatest suffering and rejection that the social sin of the human community can inflict upon the unfortunate. Jesus as God's word of compassion enters progressively into those domains of injustice, oppression and evil in which the compassion of God is most needed.

[3]See, *e.g.*, Sobrino, *op. cit.*, Chapter 1.

The movement of Jesus into this conclusion of his extraordinary life and ministry is also quite consistent in another respect with all that went before. A special character of his personality and attitudes that all had remarked upon was his simplicity in human relations which undercut all the distortions caused by abuse of authority and status and by various kinds of role playing to meet false expectations and standards of society. He had never shown any desire for status or honors himself and had associated with equal readiness with the privileged and with the disreputable, careless of the aura of sin which his association with the latter cast around him in the eyes of the respectable and pious. His interest had always been in the simply human reality of the women and men and children around him, and he had presented himself to them as simply human, rejecting titles and speculations about himself as well as the attempt to confer a royal role upon him.

In the account of his arrest, trial and execution, he follows this through consistently. Even in the arrest and trial he speaks as one free man to another, indeed as though God alone reigned in human society and there were no consequences to fear. He does not offer a defense in the trial, as though he has no need to make his case before this court, but he also suffers the consequences stripped of any claim to special protection or consideration. Jesus crucified is a naked man among the stripped and unprotected of the world who cannot clothe themselves in the privileges of power. And that is his last word to us. He died as he lived, among the poor and disregarded and unprivileged by his own choice. In death as in life, he presents himself as simply human, not defined in terms of status or power over others, simply a human being speaking out of his own vision of God and the world and the meaning of life, to share that vision and the hope arising out of it with other human persons.

The vision of Jesus and the hope arising out of it could not have been shared by force of compulsion of others, by external sanctions of power such as the world knows power. It could not have come about in that way because it was a vision of reconciliation and communion with God and with one another at a very profound level of human freedom and spontaneity. It was a vision before which all power is as nothing, a vision that could be shared only by invitation and by respecting the freedom of the others in hope, in patience, in perseverance and in ultimate vulnerability.

From any standpoint of human wisdom, Jesus gambled with his own ultimate vulnerability as the high stakes of the game and lost. He lost not only his life and his personal reputation but he lost the achievement of the dream that certainly meant more to him than his life. If we grant that he engaged in a serious process of human discernment and decision at all, then he must surely have wondered sometimes in those last days or hours whether he had been right to press the matter of the immediacy of the Reign of God so urgently, confronting the people with a choice and a leap of faith which they were so obviously not ready to make. By any ordinary standard of human wisdom, the career of Jesus was a failure, and he died knowing it. He died knowing that the only glimmer of hope for his dream was that his closest friends, who had understood so little of it, would grasp the word of God spoken to them in his death better than they had been able to hear it in his life. That he really entertained this hope seems to be evidenced by the legacy of the Eucharist which he left to his followers, inviting them back across history and cultural and linguistic chasms to enter again into the mystery of his death of defeat and try to read it as a new Exodus.[4]

This leads to that third question concerning the sense in which this death can possibly have been "allowed" by God, and can possibly be seen as salvific. As has been pointed out often enough in contemporary theological literature, the death of Jesus by crucifixion, concluding his mission in failure, requires us to rethink in the most radical terms our whole understanding of God and of the relationship of God to creation.[5] It turns upside down our more usual understanding of the omnipotent God, master of the universe, lord of history, whose will is always accomplished. It suggests the curious theme of the powerlessness of God before the self-destruction of human sin.

In itself, the death of Jesus is not only his failure, but the failure of the transcendent creator-God. And yet, the death of Jesus is redemptive. The curious Christian tradition of redemption or atonement by "paying off the ransom" may have used images and arguments that became legalistic and petty. It is repugnant to think of the pain of Jesus as ransom money paid to the devil to get the human race out of his power, though the model had its basis in analogy with human situations that were all too real. Likewise it is repugnant to think of the suffering of Jesus as compensation paid to God for the offense to God's majesty expressed in human sinning—a compensation that re-establishes amicable relationships between the divine and human parties—although this also

[4]*Cf.* Joachim Jeremias, *The Eucharistic Words of Jesus* (N.Y.: Scribners, 1966)

[5]*Cf.* Jurgen Moltmann, *The Crucified God* (N.Y.: Harper & Row, 1974) which is entirely devoted to this theme.

reflects patterns of human justice actually in force in society. But, in spite of the repugnant nature of the way these analogies were formulated, there is obviously an important insight underlying them.

Both the life and the death of Jesus reverse in a basic and total way that distortion of human life and society which is the disorientation of sin. Sin in its most basic sense, as pictured in the story of the garden, is a seizure of the controls that ought to be in God's disposition. It is a placing of self at the center and focus of life and history, an attempt to construct the world to one's own specifications. It is an attempt to seize an unlimited, unsituated freedom in disregard of others and in forgetfulness of the ultimate claims of God as creator and final goal of life. Sin disrupts the garden, that is the harmony of creation which makes it a habitable, hospitable place, because it attempts to reorganize it around another center.

Sin has become the condition of human life in history. The consequences of evil deeds haunt us down the centuries with their reverberating echoes. They become hardened into standard expectations and patterns of behavior, into the structures of society that are seen as the guarantees of the good. Sin incarnates itself in every kind of violence and compulsion and disguises itself often under the masks of law and order in society—ways of stabilizing and maintaining oppressive power and privilege for those who already possess it. Sin expresses itself in fears and suspicion and hatred ill-disguised. It leaves its deposits in prejudices, rivalries, quest of security in the hoarding of goods and the claiming of privilege to the disadvantage of others. It emerges constantly in an irrational lust for power to compel other human beings and shape the world to one's own imaginings.

The life and death of Jesus reveal to us in startling ways how pervasive in our world is sin. They reveal this because Jesus lived and died by very different criteria of the good and the desirable and even of the possible in human relations. Jesus lived as though God were at the center of reality for all of us, as though we all recognized God as the final goal. Jesus relativised all else to the welcoming of God into his creation as rightful ruler and lawgiver, but in a sense remote from our usual ideas of ruling power. Jesus left the world forever changed by the haunting memory of his unrealized dream. He appealed to no authorities. He did not need to make such an appeal. His good news of the accessibility and inner coherence of God's Reign in human affairs is self-validating in the consciousness of human persons, answering an existential need, and it becomes more and more convincingly self-validating in proportion as people respond and begin to live by it in any measure whatsoever.

It is in this sense that the failure of Jesus is turned upside down and becomes the triumph of God's word of hope and consolation into the world. It is in this sense that our understanding of the transcendent God is transformed. The God who appears as powerless against the self-destruction of human sin when we expect divine action as coming from outside human freedom, becomes God-with-us in the divine word of compassion spoken in the person of Jesus, transforming the human dilemma from within human freedom in such a way that the human community can be rallied in solidarity with the response of Jesus to the human situation.

7

The Resurrection of Jesus and the
Imitation of Christ

The Resurrection is not something easily understood or
explained by hearsay. It is the testimony of believers naming
an experience for those who share it. It is clear that what has
happened is utterly unlike anything else in their experience
and that there is no language, no imagery, no symbolism that
can do justice to the event. It is also clear that they do not
venture to attempt any statement at all about what the
Resurrection was like for Jesus, that is to say how he experienced the Resurrection. They testify and preach and write
only about their own experience of the event. Yet this certainly does not imply that they refer to some type of vision or

realization which has happened to them without anything happening in the experience of Jesus himself. The testimony suggests that they would have rejected this interpretation vehemently.

Because they are attempting to testify concerning an event utterly unlike any other experience they have had or have heard of others having, they search for a symbolism in their scriptures and traditions that might at least hint at the reality of which they speak. We know that they find basically two kinds of imagery—the imagery of exaltation of Jesus by God and the imagery which came in time to be the standard language, that of being raised from the dead.[1] In both these images, the event that has already happened to Jesus and among his followers is represented in a language that is strongly eschatological. There is, in other words, an unmistakable claim that the end-time of Jewish hope, the promised Reign of God has broken in on the human situation through the person of Jesus. The truly controversial message in the Jewish context of the time appears to be this eschatological implication which is carried by the imagery used. If God has raised Jesus, then the promised Reign of God has been initiated, but this blatantly contradicts the apparent total failure of the mission of Jesus in his death by crucifixion.

The real question about the Resurrection of Jesus is not the question concerning what the experience of it was for Jesus, nor even the question whether the tomb was indeed empty,

---

[1] For contrasting conclusions on the resurrection accounts as seen by New Testament scholars, see Raymond Brown, *The Virginal Conception and Bodily Resurrection of Jesus* (N.Y.: Paulist, 1973), and Willi Marxsen, *The Resurrection of Jesus of Nazareth*, translated by Margaret Kohl (Philadelphia: Fortress, 1970). *Cf.* also H. A. Williams, *True Resurrection* (N.Y.: Holt, Rinehart & Winston, 1972).

nor whether Thomas touched flesh and blood wounds with his hands. The real question has to do with God's self-revelation in Jesus and whether anything had really changed in the human situation through the death of Jesus and the inbreaking of the divine in history in consequence of the life and death of Jesus. This is the question as to what we really mean by calling Jesus saviour—the crucial question of a Christology.

When the earliest followers of Jesus were asked to substantiate their claims for him, their principal answer (according to the narratives in the Acts of the Apostles) appears to have been to point to the transformation in the community and to invite reflection on the self-validating quality of this transformation. Their accounts are not explanations for what had happened but rather simply statements of what had happened, which they confidently attributed to the person of Jesus and to the power and Spirit of God acting in Jesus. It is clear that any understanding of the mystery of the Resurrection must come by way of reflection on the praxis of living in the community and Spirit of the Risen Christ.

This experience of the Resurrection in the life of the community of believers is not limited to the first witnesses though these obviously had a special role, having been participant in the preaching ministry of Jesus and in the tragedy of his death. The New Testament itself emphasizes that the immediate experience of the Resurrection, that is of the Risen Christ, was open to new-comers. Such, for instance, is the case with Saul of Tarsus, realizing that in the followers of the Way whom he persecutes he is in touch with the very person of Jesus. What this means for subsequent generations, including our own, is that the Resurrection is not, or should not be, a matter of hearsay evidence for us, but a matter of direct experience.

The claim that is made for Jesus by Christians is not, of course, a claim of a simple resuscitation. Jesus is not brought back to the same life which he left. The claim is of a transformation, a breakthrough, to a wholly new mode of existence. When we look for clues as to what this wholly new mode or existence is, we find first of all the assurance that it is unconquerable, unquenchable, invulnerable, deathless. Indeed it is not only of the Risen Jesus that it is said that he has conquered death, but it is claimed that in some significant way death no longer holds sway over the followers of Jesus. The striking statement in the letter to the Hebrews (2:14-15) is that Jesus by his death broke the power of him who had death at his command, liberating all those who all their lives had been enslaved by their fear of death.

This seems to be a very important clue to the meaning of the claim of salvation in Jesus that Christians have made from the beginning. It is in this sense of the overcoming of death, by a liberation from the fear of death that holds us enslaved all through our lifetime, that Christian tradition since early patristic times has honored the martyrs and celebrated their deaths as moments of triumph for them and for the community. Again, in our own days, this type of response is heard from Third World situations concerning the deaths of those who have spoken for the poor and oppressed at the cost of their lives, and of those who have worked among the abandoned and marginated knowing that they invited persecution and violence against themselves by doing so.

For the community of believers the Resurrection of Jesus is experienced as a great deliverance or liberation, primarily from crippling fear of persecution, rejection and death. It is also celebrated as a deliverance from a stunted and fettered imagination that could not look beyond the existing prejudices and rivalries and hostilities, nor envisage any exit from an endless spiral of violence. It is celebrated, in other words, as a freeing of the imagination with explosive force to embrace possibilities for human life in peace and non-violence and in communities of creative reconciliation. Nothing that pertains to the Reign of God in human society is unthinkable any more, and there is a momentum of hope and courage to implement the visions of hitherto undreamed of possibilities—a momentum that can only be attributed to a breakthrough of power.

This kind of overcoming of death, by the conquest of the fear of death, is central to the entire issue of redemption from sin. If sin is essentially that disorientation which is constituted by a self-centered life, by an unwillingness to acknowledge mutual dependence, and by dogged persistence in trying to create the world to one's own specifications in disregard of the existence and freedom and destiny of other human persons, then death to the sinner is ultimate annihilation, total defeat, final frustration. And then the legacy of sin and sinfulness in the world is bound to be compounded by the things that people will do and will endorse in order to hold their personal deaths at bay. To find and acknowledge one's goal and meaning in life as something beyond oneself, beyond one's own survival, is to experience liberation from the crushing burden of that desperate fear of death. Nothing can be so liberating to the ability of a human person to live fully in the present and to live in peace and constructive harmony with others as the ability to acknowledge and accept one's own mortality with trust in and surrender to God.

Again and again in history heroes have sacrificed their own lives for others, in battle, in rescue operations, and in many other ways. There is always a certain nobility and grace in this that has a freeing and enhancing effect on the quality of life for that person up to death, and has an exhilarating, uplifting effect on the witnesses. Such a death is frequently celebrated with more pride and gratitude and joy than sorrow. Such is the community's claim for Jesus. But the claim goes far beyond this also. It is a claim that the empowering, life giving, hope inspiring, revelatory death of Jesus is potentially universal in its uplifting and transforming of human lives and human society. Christians claim this, not because it can somehow be demonstrated from history, but because of their experience of the power in their own lives and their recognition of it as going to the root of human need and human possibility. This seems to be the existential base of the claim that there is one name given us under heaven by which all may be saved.

Conquest of death by the overcoming of the fear of death, however, is not the only way in which Christians have traditionally described the power of the Resurrection in their lives. Another favorite way of expressing it is in terms of a birth into a new life, and particularly a rebirth into community as in the first letter of Peter (1:22-24) where it is also described as a rebirth into living hope, and into an inheritance that cannot spoil or wither (1:3-5). This experience of rebirth into living hope, into an indestructible inheritance, in a community of quite transformed relations between persons and groups, has been expressed just as vividly in our own times by members of the "basic Christian communities," members of charismatic groups, members of social action and liberation movements in the name of Christ. It is a testimony of being liberated oneself so as to become in turn the liberation of others.

At the root of both these experiences and expressions—that which is concerned with the conquest of the fear of death and that which has to do with the rebirth into a radically new experience of community—is a startlingly new experience of God. Perhaps the most fundamental meaning of the Resurrection for Christians is the challenge to recognize God in a quite new way. The power of God is recognized as the direct inversion of what we ordinarily think of as power, for we take our model of power from mechanical motion of material objects. We see it as the ability to compel others by applying sanctions, sanctions that are extrinsic to the issue and to the persons concerned. What appears as the power of God is quite the inverse—ability to share wisdom with others, to invite by the intrinsic sanction of the fittingness, the wholesomeness, the beatific character of what is being proposed.

The whole preaching of Jesus concerning the coming Reign of God emphasized this quality of essential non-violence.[2] The rule of God is not by compulsion, that is by extrinsic sanctions, but rather by sharing of vision and wisdom and purpose, by invitation and patient waiting upon the freedom of those invited. That which constituted the tragedy of the ministry of Jesus, also constituted its most coherent statement, for in response to rejection, Jesus did not resort to violence, not even to subtle violence to people's consciences and freedom. He stood his ground in the witness he personally had to give, as

[2]Some scholars have disputed that the teaching and personal stance of Jesus were non-violent in principle, but it is very difficult to put any other construction on the well-known sayings concerning meekness, forgiveness and non-retaliation.

speaking the compassionate and longing word of God into the human situation, and for this he was crucified. But he spoke the compassionate word of God into the world in all the truth of its non-violent respect for the free response of those who were not yet ready to respond, for it was only his death which set free in them the power to respond. And because of this God raised him from death, giving him a name above every name, a name in which all might be saved from the confusion and frustration of a sinful history under the crushing spell of the fear of death.

It is this many-faceted compassion of Jesus that offers the key to the Resurrection. It is a compassion that goes out to every kind of human suffering both in healing and in challenge, a compassion that respects the freedom and patiently invites response from those who are unfree, gently liberating them by affirmation and respect and expectation. But it is also a compassion in a more radical sense in that he enters into the situation of their suffering, the situation of their enslavement to sin and fear and frustration. He enters into it all the way to the bitter end, an ever present and most extraordinary companion in the human dilemma and the diabolic trap. He redeems the situation of hopelessness by being there, because where he is is after all not quite hopeless.

This is the power of Jesus, but it is most typically the power of God, though our thinking and imagining has had to be turned upside down by the encounter with Jesus to recognize it. In acting this way Jesus acts divinely, and in acting this way Jesus embodies his own experience of intimacy with God in such a way that in the encounter with him that experience becomes ours. The Resurrection of Jesus is above all else the revelation and the realization of God-with-us, and the token of it is that the presence of Jesus has become interior to our consciousness, interior to our freedom, not doing things for us as we remain passive but empowering us.

In the total self-gift of his compassion, Jesus acts most divinely, yet it is in the same compassion that he becomes in his Resurrection most imitable. To be a follower of Jesus means in the first place to enter by compassion into his experience, with all that it expresses of the divine and of the human. And it means in the second place to enter with him into the suffering and the hope of all human persons, making common cause with them as he does, and seeking out as he does the places of his predilection among the poor and despised and oppressed. This would seem to be the meaning of Eucharist and the meaning of Church.

8

Jesus, The Compassion of God

The Christian claim for Jesus goes beyond all that has been stated so far in this book. Christian faith proclaims that Jesus is divine. Contemporary problems with that statement do not concern its truth but its intelligibility, as explained in the introduction. The question for Christology today is how to express the relation of Jesus to the transcendent God in fidelity to the tradition and in a way that can make sense to the contemporary believer. This is really a task of showing how the divinity claim arises out of the believers' experience of salvation in Jesus Christ, and of expressing the claim in imagery and analogies that speak to the contemporary sense of reality. The first part of this has been attempted in the three foregoing chapters. The second part will be attempted in this chapter.

The Christology of the New Testament has a remarkable plurality, so much so that one ought perhaps to speak of Christologies in the plural.[1] Within the New Testament itself there is no apparent attempt to reconcile and combine them into a single perspective. Various models or analogies are used to relate Jesus to the transcendent God. There is the mode of address as *kyrios*, Lord. There are the Johannine images that recall the creation story of Genesis 1, namely Word of God, spoken into the world, and Light of God shining into the world (later found in the creedal formulation, "light from light"), as well as Truth and Life. Also obviously echoing the imagery of Genesis 1, but with particular reference to the creation of human persons, is the language of the Pauline tradition. Probably quoting an earlier hymn using Hebrew expressions of divine wisdom, Colossians 1:15-20 presents Jesus as the visible image of the invisible God, the pattern of creation, the one in whom the divine came to dwell.

Besides the images that refer to the creation stories of Genesis, there are images with reference rather specifically to Jesus as the "power and wisdom of God" (I Corinthians 1:24), and even the implied representation of Jesus as the true Law of God which seems to be pervasive in Pauline thought. Further there are scattered images of Jesus, such as the Way to the Father, life-giving Spirit, and so forth, besides many others not of immediate interest here, because their function is to relate Jesus to human history and destiny rather than directly to the transcendent God.

[1] *Cf.* James D.G. Dunn, *Christology in the Making* (Philadelphia: Westminster, 1980), *passim*, but especially "Conclusion," pp. 251-268.

All of these images relating Jesus to the transcendent God—Word, Light, Truth, Life, Image, Pattern, Dwelling, Power, Wisdom, Law, Way, Spirit—are impersonal. They are all, so to speak, verbs in disguise. They represent the "activity" of God, and express an outreach of God to or into creation. In themselves they do not address the question of a pre-existence,[2] though they certainly lend themselves to that understanding concerning Jesus. They offer the possibility of envisaging pre-existence in terms that are at once personal and non-restrictive. They are personal because they express activities that imply personal relationships, personal participation. They are non-restrictive because they do not require the imagination to project into eternity some kind of reflection of a human person, which must then be qualified with all kinds of negations—no bodiliness, no temporality, and so forth.

The New Testament attribution of divinity to Jesus appears in the first place to have been linked with the Resurrection, later with the baptism in the Jordan by John, later yet with the conception and birth, and finally in John's Gospel with the pre-existence of Jesus. The New Testament does not seem to require that the "divinization" of Jesus or, as we should say, the Incarnation, can only be seen as a moment at the inception of life, a moment preceding any human response and therefore totally independent of it. Rather it seems to allow for the paradox which names those four different moments— Resurrection, Baptism, birth, and pre-existent eternity—

[2]*ibid.* It may be objected that the references in the present chapter deliberately omit Philippians 2:6-11. For argument that this Pauline text bears reference to Adam created in the divine image, and therefore is not an assertion of personal pre-existence in a divine nature, see Dunn, *op. cit.,* pp. 114-121.

precisely because the mystery of the Incarnation can be approached from different viewpoints.

There is, however, in the New Testament another image which subsequent tradition seems to have developed most. It is the image of the Son of God, an image which in its Biblical setting does not necessarily involve a divinity claim. It is easy to know why this image should come to dominate the scene. The so-called "Abba-experience" of Jesus[3] is so pervasive in all the testimonies about him that, in the context of his intimacy with God as Father, nothing could be more natural than to think of Jesus primarily as the Son of God. The Prologue to John's Gospel does this, when it states that God's Word, which was with God in the beginning, which was what God was, the Word by which God created, (so far using the image of the Word simply for the activity of God), became human, dwelling among us so that we saw in him a glory befitting the Father's only Son (using the personal image of the Son as subsequent to the Incarnation).

Even in John's Gospel, the imagination of the devout reader is not really required to project into eternity a personal pre-existence of the Son beside the Father.[4] There is an easy ambiguity here that is very much in keeping with traditional Jewish ways of having Wisdom and Torah somehow dwelling and conversing with God in God's own transcendent realm outside of human history. This, of course, is what might be

---

[3] *Cf.* Joachim Jeremias, *op. cit.*

[4] *Cf.* Dunn, *op. cit.* pp. 239-250. Dunn evidently considers the whole history of Christology as a struggle to come to terms with John's Gospel, yet he really does not explain at any point of his lengthy discussion why he sees the imagery of John as necessarily implying personal pre-existence. Dunn's method seems to yield the same results with John's images as with those of the synoptics.

expected in view of the Hebrew emphasis on the unity of God, which would hardly allow the devout imagination to place a person there but could tolerate the literary personification of God's attributes.

Subsequent Christian reflection, while taking the impersonal imagery as metaphorical, seems to have taken the image of the Son more literally, and therefore more restrictively, than was intended, and seems to have taken it for granted that the text of Scripture itself compelled us to this. Indeed, even when the discussions of the fourth and fifth centuries centered upon the role of the *Logos* in relation to the transcendent God and in relation to Jesus, there is often a hint that it is not the image of God's utterance but the image of God's Son that is being projected into eternity.[5]

It seems to be the unspoken assumption that this image is not as strictly metaphorical as the others, which causes the trouble of intelligibility to many contemporary believers. Aware that to speak of God as person is metaphor or analogy taken from the observation of human individuals, and aware that to speak of Three Persons in God is therefore a densely compounded metaphor, believers naturally want to ask what kind of statement is being made when we represent Jesus as personally pre-existent. If we are taking "person" literally, then we mean human person. But in that case we cannot speak of pre-existence because the claim does not concern the humanity of Jesus but the divinity. But if we speak of the pre-existence of Jesus as divine Person, then we are not speaking of the literal meaning of the word "person," but of

---

[5]For a full account of the process of the Christological accounts, giving extensive primary sources, see Richard A. Norris, *The Christological Controversy* (Philadelphia: Fortress, 1980).

the analogy by which we can refer to God in personal terms, compounded by the highly specialized, technical sense of the term "divine Person" as used in trinitarian discourse. In other words, in this case we are not really speaking of personal pre-existence in any sense which imagination or common sense would recognize as personal. To the theologian this may be subtlety. To the devout layperson of lively intelligence and inquiring turn of mind, it is frustration and confusion and does not tend to further prayer or Christian living.

The question will, of course, arise whether this discussion is academic and somewhat impertinent in both senses of the word, in the context of the definition and legacy of Chalcedon. Therefore, it is important to consider carefully the parameters which Chalcedon imposes on further discussion of Christology.[6] The declared intent of the fathers of Chalcedon was to exhort and encourage all Christians to join together in peace and harmony among themselves in their confession of faith in Christ. Such a confession, they declared, must be true to the sources of our tradition as we have them in the scriptures, the formulae of public worship (that is the liturgy), the standard catechesis of the churches, and the explicit teaching of the church fathers gathered in previous great councils. The Tome of Leo, which is included specifically in the defined teaching of Chalcedon, gathers up a great range of the traditional imagery and language, tolerant of a considerable variety of approaches as long as they can be reconciled with the language and imagery of Scripture and worship.

---

[6]For a full logical and rhetorical analysis of Chalcedon and its implications, see Frans Jozef van Beeck, *Christ Proclaimed: Christology as Rhetoric* (N.Y.: Paulist, 1979).

This reconciliation with the traditional language and imagery, as Chalcedon was concerned to demand it, seems to have as its most basic purpose to preserve the paradox of our Christology in such a way that Jesus can be worshipped without idolatry and imitated in truth, not in a kind of pious fiction. Expressed more abstractly, Chalcedon was concerned to guarantee the true humanity of Jesus against monophysite interpretations, which envisaged the humanity as simply disappearing or dissolving into the divinity at the Incarnation. Yet Chalcedon also wanted to be faithful to Christian piety as already officially expressed at Nicea, Constantinople and Ephesus—a tradition which had doggedly maintained the true divinity of Jesus, even while it was manifestly incapable of giving a coherent rational explanation of what was meant by the claim.

The reason for the Christian clinging to this paradoxical statement of the one Jesus who is truly human as we are as well as being truly divine as the transcendent Father and Creator is, seems to be based quite solidly in a critical reflection on Christian praxis. On the one hand the radical transformation of human possibilities, as experienced in the community of Christians, can only be the re-creating, redeeming power of the divine, and Christians have no shadow of doubt that this power comes out from the Risen Jesus. On the other hand, the Jesus in whom they place their unconditional trust, and in whom they encounter the divine face to face, is the Jesus of history, a man like other men, historically and socially situated in a world of sin and struggle, one who lived his life in the same human situation as other human persons, and with whom there can be genuine solidarity.

There seems to be a central soteriological concern in this. If a God in disguise did what Jesus did and "suffered" what Jesus suffered, this could but be a charade, and it would be difficult to see in what way the human situation would really have changed in consequence of his "life" and "death." Yet there is also a concern to establish that the break-through that has occurred in Jesus for the whole human community is more than a great act of human valor and generosity. Such acts have occurred before and will occur again, but they do not have the character of definitively changing the possibilities of the human situation. Only the breakthrough of the divine redeeming power could radically change the human situation within a sinful world and history. Only the breakthrough of the divine compassion within human freedom could really do that. Such, in a modern restatement, seems to be the soteriological concern of Chalcedon.

There is, of course, also a strictly theological concern in the task of Chalcedon, that is the task of guaranteeing the humanity of Jesus within an accepted tradition of his divinity. That concern is to avoid simply identifying Jesus with God, the Creator and the transcendent, with all that would imply of the loss of transcendence and the restriction of the being of God. Moreover, this concern is practical for Christian tradition inasmuch as the New Testament and the formulae of Christian prayer define Jesus precisely by his relationship to the Father. Yet, if Jesus is not simply to be identified as God, he is at the same time not to be put beside the Father as another god (for the Christian community has always said on the basis of its own praxis that the monotheism of Israel is the truth of the divine) and not to be considered as an intermediate being between the strictly divine and the properly human (as established at Nicea).

Beyond the soteriological and theological concerns, there is the even more important, strictly practical concern of Christian spirituality. Christian spirituality is based on the assumption that to place ultimate trust in Jesus and the following of his Way is not wrong or misleading, and that to make an unconditional surrender of one's life and being to Jesus is not idolatrous. At the center of the Christian understanding of revelation and redemption stands the person of Jesus. Of him we say that he not only brings us the revelation of God, but that in his person he is the revelation of God. This is a very broad claim, for it means that the ultimate touchstone of truth in the human encounter with God is not any formulation in words but a person, and that in case of perplexity in new situations and confronted with new questions, one's access to discernment is not rational extrapolation from a previous statement but attentive presence to, and imitation of, a person.

This last concern is evidently the foundation and reason of the other two. What is truly important in the language of Christology is that it be faithful to the service of Christian life, prayer and action in the world, making it possible to discern what is truly redemptive in a changing historical situation. There seems to be nothing in the purpose or in the verbal formulation of Chalcedon (with its plurality of canonized former expressions) that requires us to take a language of personal pre-existence as immediately appropriate to the reality rather than as part of a multi-faceted, highly paradoxical presentation of a mystery that cannot be neatly captured in rational explanations.[7]

---

[7]Cf. Norris, *op. cit.*, pp. 29-31; and van Beeck, *op. cit.*, pp. 129-135.

Although it seems to have been so understood by post-Chalcedonian discussion, there does not seem to be any good reason for concluding that Chalcedon itself intended to imply that the "one person" on which it insists is to be understood as a pre-existent divine person, thus locating the reality of Jesus very firmly outside the human. In the first place, it cannot be understood in this way because Chalcedon is using the term "person" in a highly specialized sense, that is, to capture the unknown content that identifies the divine and the human in Jesus. We, on the other hand, use the word "person" to designate any individual of the human species, with particular emphasis on those qualities of the human species that are involved in a reflective self-awareness that is the basis for memory and for spontaneity. Moreover, Chalcedon, concerned as it was, to deny the monophysite position, quite certainly did not intend to deny Jesus full humanity including that human self-awareness which grounds human memory and human spontaneity. As a matter of historical fact, the further councils of antiquity continued the project of Chalcedon by insisting on a human will, human spontaneity and so forth.[8]

It would seem, therefore, that in the light of all the foregoing considerations, fidelity to Chalcedon in our contemporary situation is observed in two ways. There is the concern to maintain for Christian understanding the dynamic tension between the language and imagery of Bible, worship and traditional teaching on the one hand and the language and imagery of the contemporary perception of reality on the

---

[8]There are also, of course, some quite different ways of resolving the problem caused by the word, "person," such as that of Schillebeeckx, *Jesus* (N.Y.: Seabury, 1979), Part IV.

other hand. There is also the concern to maintain for Christian spirituality the dynamic tension between the worship and unconditional trust of Jesus Christ as the place of encounter with the divine in history on the one hand, and the whole-hearted commitment to the following of Christ and solidarity with him in the redemptive transformation of the whole human experience on the other hand. Fidelity to the testimonies of the New Testament would seem to require something more, namely to keep alive that ambiguity that allows a dynamic tension between the personal and impersonal in the imaging of the relation of Jesus to the transcendent God.

There can be no question, of course, of displacing the biblical images around which Christian faith has been built for so many centuries and in so many cultures and languages, expressing itself in the visual arts as well as in literature of many kinds. These images provide the thread of continuity and therefore provide a crucial means of access to the sources of our faith in the historical Christ event and the testimony of the first followers of Jesus who knew him in the flesh. That is a heritage no Christian would wish to relinquish. Further, there can be no question of setting aside Chalcedon, nor anything of the legacy of doctrinal definitions formally proposed to the church, for these are the outcome of a discernment process in the community of believers which makes us heirs to the cumulative Christian praxis and reflection on praxis of the Christian centuries. There can only be question of extending the process and of freeing the Christian imagination for a more living and integrated appropriation of the heritage of faith that is handed on.

The New Testament imagery is in itself powerful and flexible although subsequent usage has sometimes given it an alien rigidity. Jesus as the Word of God spoken in eternity and spoken now into history, is personal in the sense that it is God speaking, not in the sense that a person is envisaged in eternity in addition to God. Moreover, it allows easy passage of the imagination from the creative speaking of God in Genesis to the redemptive, recreative speaking of God in the Christ event, while resonating with memories of the Word of God as spoken by the prophets. It allows for both continuity and uniqueness in the understanding of the person and mission of Jesus, inasmuch as we are all called to be words of God to one another and to our societies and inasmuch as there have always been outstanding persons in history who have surely been words of God in a special way, while the claim is made on the other hand that Jesus is wholly identified with the divine Word or self-utterance of God. Beyond this, it allows for a helpful ambiguity in the identification, making it possible at one and the same time for Jesus to become divine as he becomes human (in the whole extent of his life from conception to Resurrection) and yet to have been the divine Word from the beginning. Once we remove the restrictions subsequently superimposed on the image of the Word, whereby the personal identity and continuity of consciousness of the human Jesus is understood to pre-exist in eternity, the paradox of becoming what he was from the beginning, namely the Word of God, is quite tolerable to the imagination because we have many analogies for it. For instance, we become what we were from the beginning, namely human.

Something similar may be said of the image of the Light and of the various other New Testament images that speak of the meaning and identity of Jesus and of his relationship to the Father. With more subtle nuances, something similar may be said of the image of the Son. Yet in all of these instances, there has been a certain freezing of the images and a chilling paralysis of the imagination as it comes in contact with them. That is why it seems urgent to suggest some further representations that arise clearly out of the contemporary Christian praxis and a critical reflection upon it.

Perhaps the representation that suggests itself most persuasively in our times is that of Jesus as the incarnate Compassion of God. Compassion is a broad term and a broad concept whose connotations and further possibilities keep reverberating. We commonly use it as synonymous with pity and it certainly means that but also more than that. It implies a movement towards the other to help, but also a movement into the experience of the other to be present in solidarity and communion of experience. It implies sensitivity, vulnerability to be affected by the experience of the other but it also implies remedial action against suffering and oppression. Most of all, it implies involvement in the situation.[9]

To speak of Jesus as the Compassion of God is to reflect on contemporary Christian praxis and on the realization that the following of Jesus in our times confronts us constantly with human suffering on a massive scale, caused by structures of society which are the solidified deposits of the consequences of

---

[9]The idea of Jesus embodying the compassion of God was proposed in a somewhat different way by Kazoh Kitamori, *The Theology of the Pain of God* (Richmond: John Knox, 1965). The Japanese original, *Kami No Itami No Shingaku*, published in 1958, was written in the aftermath of the anguish of Hiroshima and Nagasaki. It describes basically a mysticism of seeking divine communion with human suffering. What is being proposed in the present volume differs from Kitamori mainly in that it suggests activity as well as passivity, and in that it is concerned to reconcile the formulation with Chalcedon's dogmatic definition of the identity of Jesus.

evil deeds in the world. As we face these massive problems of humanly produced human suffering, there is always a sense of our own powerlessness and insignificance. Yet there is also the experience that where social sin abounds, there also "social grace" abounds even more. As Christians we do experience the rebirth of hope and courage and we do witness in our own times in places of greatest oppression and deprivation the inexplicable transforming power of basic Christian communities. We realize that the power and presence of this transformation is that of the living Risen Christ and that its quality is compassion in all the dimensions mentioned above. Then we realize that we must name Jesus Compassion, but a Compassion which in its range and power and discernment is divine.

In the contemporary Christian reflection on Christian praxis there is an ever-threatening possibility of a deep schism of affections and loyalties between those who see the liberation of the oppressed in concrete historical dimensions as central to the redemption and those who see the conflictual quality of liberation movements as contrary to the redemption which they envisage as primarily a matter of communion with and surrender to God in individual lives. The representation of Jesus as the Compassion of God seems to offer a mediation between these two perceptions of what is at stake in our practical response to the redemption, for compassion is essentially non-violent, tending to communion and community, and yet is also essentially active, tending to redress injuries and injustices.

In terms of the classic formulations of Christology, to name Jesus the Compassion of God is to preserve that balance between the personal and the impersonal that make the imaging of the incarnation possible. The Compassion of God, like the Word and the Life and the Light, refers to "activity" in God. That is to say it enables us to imagine the one God in dynamic ways. Moreover, it pictures God in "activity" that relates God to the creation and to creatures as well as to the redemption of the human race and its history. It identifies Jesus with that outreach into creation which makes God present in it, participant in it, entering into the human experience in solidarity with human suffering, history and destiny. It is a way of saying that in the person of Jesus, God truly enters into creation, into the human dilemma in all its tragic dimensions. And all of these implications seem to be facets of the traditional Christology.

Finally, to speak of Jesus as the Compassion of God allows for human initiative in Jesus in every phase of a redemptive incarnation without any denial of the divine initiative. It allows for the progressive human identification with the redemptive initiative of God so that the human Jesus becomes wholly one with the divine compassion and therefore becomes truly divine without contradiction either of the unity and transcendence of God or of the authentic humanity of Jesus.

Part III
The Believer's Christ
In A Pluralistic World

9

The Buddha and the Christ:
Detachment and Liberation

The comparison between the Buddha and Jesus, both in their life stories and in their teachings, are so striking that around the turn of the century several books were written making this comparison in some detail and sometimes going so far as to try to demonstrate that Jesus, or at least his early disciples, were actually influenced by Buddhism.[1] This chapter does not make any claim of a direct historical connection,

---

[1]E.g. Arthur Lillie, *The Influence of Buddhism on Primitive Christianity* (N.Y.: Scribner, 1893); and Dwight Goddard, *Was Jesus influenced by Buddhism?* (Thetford, Vt., 1927, publisher not identified).

nor does it claim a systematic comparison of the two. It has the far more modest intention of reflecting on some insights to be gained concerning Jesus as Christ or Savior by noting these powerful similarities with the Buddha.

As has often been noted, Buddhism is not in the strict sense a religion, for it does not (in its purer forms) worship a God. Yet it is undoubtedly a teaching of a way of salvation, and it is as such that it offers a comparison with Christianity, a comparison of the salvation that is claimed in Christ and the salvation that is claimed in Buddha. The legends of the Buddha seem to stress in this teaching of salvation especially deliverance from the fear of death, old age and suffering, and that the way of salvation is a way of renunciation and detachment, especially detachment from self by openness to the Truth. The effect which the Buddha had on his followers is told in the legends of his life in images and stories which bear remarkable resemblance to those of the Gospels, both as to the sayings, and in wonderful happenings.

The principal challenge that the teachings of the Buddha offer to the claims that Christians make for Jesus as Savior and Incarnation of the Divine seems to be in the analysis of the problem from which we need to be saved and in the prescription of the saving remedy. The teaching of the Four Noble Truths has it that suffering is a universal feature of the cycle of life and death, that suffering arises from cravings of various kinds, that it may therefore be extinguished by the fading away of craving by renunciation to the point of passing beyond birth and decay (into Nirvana), and that this may be done by following the Noble Eightfold Path of right understanding and right-mindedness (which are wisdom), right speech, right action and right living (which are morality), right effort, right attentiveness and right concentration (which together are concentration).

Although this is a profound mysticism that has to be practiced seriously to be understood, Buddhists have been kind enough to share with us in terms of a more common vocabulary what they themselves see as distinctive when they have had the opportunity to observe Western ways of thought.[2] In order to find release from what is understood to be the illusion of the self, Buddhists focus on a withdrawal from wordly affairs, and thus on a kind of withdrawal into the self, as our Western perception would view it. Although there are in the teachings and in the stories of the Buddha and his followers many references to compassion and to acts of kindness to others, the emphasis even in this exercise of compassion towards others appears to be on helping others to renounce inordinate desire and particularly in helping the others to see how destructive are all initiatives that are rooted in avarice, hatred, anger or delusion.

In its pure form, it is an atheistic mysticism and asceticism promising salvation by release from the selfhood of birth and decay. The imagery of salvation is in negative terms, just as the imagery of ultimate reality is in negative terms. However, all of this could be matched in Christian mysticism and asceticism,

---

[2]*Cf.*, for instance, *Buddha: Life and Teaching* (Mount Vernon, N.Y.: Peter Pauper Press, undated), which includes *The Gospel of Buddha*, translated and compiled by Paul Carus, with his own commentary, and *The Word of the Buddha*, assembled and translated by Nyanatiloka. From a scholarly perspective, *cf.* Edward Conze, *Buddhism: its Essence and Development* (N.Y.: Harper, 1959), and Ananda Kentish Coomaraswami, *Buddha and the Gospel of Buddhism* (N.Y.: University Books, 1964). For an extraordinary Western perception of liberation-salvation in Buddhism, see Hermann Hesse, *Siddhartha*, a novel, (N.Y.: New Directions, 1957).

at least in some of their manifestations. It could be matched in the Christian traditions because there seem indeed to be some very strong elements that are common. There is, for instance, a radical orientation to non-violence which finds its counterpart in the teaching of Jesus on meekness. The message of detachment as the condition for seeing truth and the condition for setting out on the way to salvation, is certainly common to both traditions.

Yet there is also a real difference in the analysis of the problem and in the prescription of the solution. There are basically two ways in which any doctrine of salvation can envisage the content of salvation; it can be a matter of saving the world or a matter of saving souls (the consciousness of individuals) out of the world. This difference in turn seems to be based on two ways of envisaging the problem from which we need to be saved: it can be seen as alienation by being involved in the world of affairs, or it can be seen as an alienation of the world of affairs by disorder. The Buddhist teaching is a challenge to us, and is attractive to many Westerners today because there is a simplicity and obvious rightness to it that fits well with our contemporary multidisciplinary awareness of the relativity of our knowledge and our experience. Morever, it articulates one aspect of Christian understanding of sin and redemption, an aspect that has become dominant for some Christians.

The attitude of Jesus, in contrast to this, is shaped by the intimacy of relationship to the ultimate as personal, concerned Father, and purposeful Creator. In continuity with his Hebrew religious background, Jesus takes history and human affairs with ultimate seriousness. They are within God's good creating and are called to respond to God in all the dimensions

and patterns of human activity in the world. The consciousness of the human person is not alienated by being in the
world of human affairs and history; that is where it ought to
be. Yet not only is the world in a state of alienation because it
is disoriented, but the individual consciousness is also alienated by being disoriented. Both world and individual need to
be redeemed. Here the imagery of salvation like the imagery of
the ultimate has a positive and above all a purposeful
character.

In the stories of the Buddha, compassion for others seems to
follow as a side effect of the path to enlightenment. In the
stories of Jesus, compassion seems to be the primary focus,
though it flows from his relationship to the transcendent God
as Father. The important question that it raises in relation to
spirituality is whether contemplation is at the heart of it or
charity, (renunciation and detachment being, of course, integral to both). The Christian position is that charity is at the
heart of it, so that the cultivation and exercise of compassion is
the foundational praxis of the faith, and that the Word of God
to us which is Jesus is a Word of Compassion, the Compassion
of God become human that we might share in it both
passively and actively.

In Christian perspective therefore, liberation of human
persons from alienation and suffering calls for active measures
of restructuring society, as well as the more contemplative
approach of questioning and refocussing desires. Christian
compassion is supposed to go out to persons in their corporeal-
ity, their historicity, their particularity and concreteness, and
in their relationality, for all of this is of God's good creating,
and all of this can be redeemed by a transformation that
reorients the many dimensions of human individual and social

existence to God as its meaning and goal. The Christian, in other words, is invited to follow the example of Jesus in works of healing, whether physical or social or psychological or spiritual, simply because all of these matter and because suffering and oppression are evil. It is not a matter of doing these things so as to perfect oneself in selflessness and good works, nor of doing them so as to lead people from the material and social to a concern with the spiritual, though both of these would be side effects of the action. But the Christian concern with salvation really takes in all these aspects and takes them all seriously.

This comparison suggests some further reflection on the way Christians envisage Jesus when they call him Messiah, Christ, the chosen and appointed Savior. Christians have frequently spoken and written in language that hails Jesus as the one and only Savior for the whole world and for the whole of history, for whom all waited until his historical coming and after whom none other is to be expected. Because Buddhism with its rather different approach is also a claimant for universal status, the figure of the Buddha stands not only as a confirmation and complement to the figure of Christ, but perhaps in some sense as a rival also. Today in our pluralistic social situation, therefore, Christians must face the claims of the Buddha and ask themselves how they are to account for them within the perspectives of Christian faith.

Clearly it is not necessary, in order to be a follower of Christ and a believer, to try to discredit the Buddha and show his claims to be false. A more modern approach has been to claim uniqueness and universality for Jesus in an inclusive rather than exclusive way, and yet that perhaps is not a satisfactory answer for the Christian, inasmuch as the claims of the Buddhists for Buddha, though different, are also inclusive.[3] Yet to claim only that Jesus offers a way of salvation to us which is one among many, is to fall short of fidelity to the classic statements about Jesus in the Bible and the tradition.

In fact, our claims for the uniqueness of the relation of Jesus to the transcendent God and to the destiny of the human race and its history, are not based upon any ability to demonstrate the truth of it by a combination of empirical verification and logical necessity. They are based upon a critical reflection on our own praxis which leads us to see transformation in Christ as potentially and aptly universal. That is to say, it leads us to see that transformation of all human society in the risen Christ is a possibility and would be truly redemptive from suffering and frustration into communion with God and community with one another. Buddhists do not see the goal of liberation in this way. It would seem that the only solution to the way we are to think about the universal claims we make is to see them as a friendly wager. It is a wager in which the game is the totality of life and history, and the stakes are human happiness and ultimate destiny.

[3]*Cf.* Paul Knitter, comparative study in Christology in relation to other world religious traditions, to be published in the near future, of which the author graciously allowed me to read some relevant sections.

10

Moses, Jesus and Muhammad:
Law and Liberation

If Buddhism challenges Christian believers in the claims they make for Jesus as the Christ and the definitive Word of God to the human community, Judaism and Islam do so even more immediately, and Christians are really compelled to give an account of their faith in dialogue with these two traditions. Both the complementarity and the rivalry is stronger with these two traditions because our three communities are grounded in the common acceptance of the Hebrew Scriptures as the revelatory word of God. We share a language of imagery and story and in that language of imagery and story we argue our interpretations of what God is saying to us in our history.[1]

---

[1] For Christian reflection on the symbolism held in common by the three traditions and their ways of using it, see James Kritzeck, *Sons of Abraham* (Baltimore: Helicon, 1965); and *cf.* Monika Hellwig, *Toward a Christian Theology of Israel After Christ* (Ann Arbor: University Microfilms, 1968).

134

Christianity exists because some Jews acclaimed Jesus as the fulfillment of the expectations of Israel, while others did not see this because they did not discern that radical transformation in the structures of the world which was to herald the final and definitive Reign of God among his people. They looked for peace, liberation from oppression, justice and harmony among themselves, and modest material well-being for all. This is what they looked for and they did not see it coming about, and indeed even today a Jew can look at the world after more than nineteen centuries of Christianity, and ask with evident justification whether anything has really changed and what, in practical terms is the meaning of the claims made for Jesus.

For many centuries Christians seem to have assumed that the messiahship of Jesus ought to be obvious to anyone who had read the Hebrew Scriptures and that therefore Jews must really be in bad faith in asking their questions so persistently through the centuries of Christian history. Even though scholarly discussion between Jews and Christians was a feature of the mediaeval period, Jews were socially and politically so much an oppressed minority, that Christians have not really understood the force of the Jewish question until our own times when the Enlightenment, the dis-establishment of Christianity and the generally secular thrust of modern thought have tended to make religious persons of all faiths allies rather than rivals. And it is in that context of friendly interest and curiosity that the Jewish questions about Jesus are being asked today.[2]

[2]*E.g.* David G. Flusser, *Jesus*, translated by Ronald Walls, (N.Y.: Herder, 1969); and Samuel Sandmel, *We Jews and Jesus* (N.Y.: Oxford University Press, 1965).

Obviously, the divinity claim for Jesus as we have often formulated it in the past, is something no Jew could take seriously as anything other than idolatry. Yet the divinity claim for Jesus was originally formulated by Jews who saw Jesus as being in the clearest continuity with the traditions and expectations of Israel. The Jewish objections to the claim as they have heard it formulated is that it denies the unity of God on which all hope and all morality and all coherent understanding of reality is based.

We ought to have been taking the Jewish objection seriously, not because Jews are making it but because they are making it on grounds that we share with them, namely the concern to acknowledge in all things the unity and the transcendent otherness of God. The force of the objection rests upon the personal pre-existence as we have tended to image it, and is further enhanced by the historical attribution of it to Jewish authorship. What Jews are telling us, seen from the Christian perspective, is that not only is this interpretation inconsistent with the unity and transcendence of God, but that we should look at it again very carefully because it is extremely unlikely, if not impossible, that this particular interpretation as subsequently appropriated was what the original followers of Jesus intended to say to us about him.

Perhaps the interpretation of Jesus as identified with, that is as Incarnating, the Compassion of God, answers this Jewish objection in a way that makes our Christian faith more internally intelligible and coherent. This is not to say that it may be expected to silence the Jewish objection, because that objection has already accumulated centuries of history and has contributed to the Jewish theology of the election of Israel as a claim that holds true even in face of the growth of Christianity and Islam.[3] It may, however, not be too much to hope that an interpretation such as has been proposed here will at least offer common ground for discussion between Jews and Christians.

This central issue that has stood between Christians and Jews is, of course, also the central issue between Christians and Muslims for whom the commitment to the unity and transcendent holiness and otherness of God is just as central as it is for the Jews. Besides this issue of the divinity claim made for Jesus, there is among all three of our faith traditions a very important issue that has been somewhat obscured by the focus on the divinity claim. This is the issue of the finality of revelation. Each of our traditions claims that the revelation which grounds it is final and definitive for the remainder of history. Thus for Israel the Mosaic covenant with its revelation of the Torah sets the stage for all that is to come and is by its very nature final in history, that is, enduring until it is fully consummated in messianic fulfillment. For Christians the Mosaic covenant was a step on the way, and Jesus in his person is the fulfillment, though we live still in the tension between the Resurrection and the *parousia* or final "coming," and therefore live suspended between what is already and what is not yet. For Muslims, both Moses with the Sinai covenant and Jesus in his ministry were steps on the way to the final revelation made to the last and greatest prophet, Muhammad.

---

[3] *Cf.* the basic Muslim profession of faith: there is no God but Allah and Muhammad is his prophet. *Cf.* the "Pillars of Islam" in the standard teaching.

This raises for Christians a question which is also from the Christian point of view a Christological question. It raises the question concerning the messianic role of Jesus and its definitive character for the rest of history — in a more insistent form, the same question with which the followers of the Baptist come to Jesus. It really compels us to ask the meaning of our claim in a pluralistic context in which it is disputed both as to its truth and as to its intelligibility. We have not taken this Christological question very seriously in the past, probably because the divinity claim with its dominant interpretation of personal pre-existence made any further consideration of the uniqueness and finality of Jesus seem unnecessary.

When we consider the question outside the kind of easy certainty provided by personal divine pre-existence as the Only Son, the question acquires far more urgency and cogency. It is demonstrable that it cannot be answered in the forum of the three religious traditions in dialogue. What really emerges from the asking of the question, is a clearer awareness of the source of our assertion and of the context that gives it meaning. The source of our assertion is the critical reflection on our own experience of living as the followers of Jesus in the community of the Risen Christ. The critique of that experience tells us that the salvific thrust of the teaching and impact of Jesus in our world cannot be exhausted in history because it goes to the root of the entire problem of human alienation or sinfulness, and would, if really and fully implemented bring about the salvation of the world.

It is evident that the convictions of Judaism and of Islam regarding the finality of their revelations arise similarly out of their reflection on the praxis of their traditions and can claim similar assurance of the truth in a similar context of reference.

This raises the question whether all might be right or whether the claims must by their nature be exclusive in such a way that only one could in truth be right. The model of Christology that has been proposed in this volume suggests that in principle all might be right and that this would be eschatologically evident in a retrospective observation of the convergence of the substance, if not of the religious language and observances, of the traditions.

However, there is also the question of the content of the traditions. There appears to be a real issue in the attitude of the three traditions towards the relation between law and liberation. In this question Israel and Islam stand over against Christianity in their expectations concerning the salvific power of the law. Historians of religion might be inclined to attribute the difference to the circumstances of the founding of the three traditions, for the Hebrews as a scattered and disorganized slave people and the Arabs as disorganized and lawless tribes were in a roughly comparable situation. Salvation from the sinfulness and alienation of their situation quite obviously required strong social structures and an explicit and detailed code of law enforced with rigor, as the prerequisite for peoplehood and the pursuit of a common purpose and ideal. Jesus, on the other hand, lived at a time when the social structures of control and the traditional observance of the Mosaic law were both over-extended.

Yet, even if this sociological and historical observation is correct, it leaves the traditions with different emphases in their teaching concerning salvation, and this becomes for Christians a Christological question also. It questions the nature of the salvation offered in Jesus and therefore the content of the claim that Jesus is savior. Both Judaism and Islam place considerable trust in the efficacy of law in reorienting the human situation towards God. At least ideally, the good society, the society of believers is a political theocracy, in which the revealed law of God is implemented as the law of the land. This means that by implication God's reign in human society is brought about by force, by sanctions that are extrinsic.

The Christian response to this, as so explicitly formulated by Paul in the New Testament, is that essentially the law of God is a law of freedom, that is a law that binds by intrinsic sanction only, which is to say that it binds by its inner wisdom and coherence. In a world and a history in which the consequences of evil deeds have been compounded into structures and tragic dilemmas, a law of extrinsic sanctions, or implementation by force, may be inescapable, but it is at best a tutor to bring individuals and societies to a maturity in which they are able to discern and respond to the law of God which is freedom. This perspective is not wholly different from the traditions of Israel in which there is also the constant reminder that it is necessary to read between the lines of the commandments and that obedience is more than execution of commands but extends into discernment of God's will. Yet the difference of emphasis is there.

In practice Christians do not deserve the strictures of those Jews and Muslims who accuse us of anti-nomianism or lawlessness, because we have been so little faithful to the proclamation of the law of Christ as freedom. Our actual history is one of many legalisms in the structuring of our churches, and of attempts at church establishment from Constantine onwards which came close to claiming to be theocracies. Moreover, those who have exercised authority in the churches in the name of Christ have frequently been not ministers but bosses. There seems therefore to be a double challenge for Christians in the traditions of Israel and of Islam. There is the questioning of our understanding that Jesus is the redemptive force in the world (the Compassion of God) because of the liberation from the tutelage of the law (which has never really been tried). But secondly, there is the question as to whether we are being quite serious and honest when we make the claim of liberation from the tutelage of the law by life in Christ.

Any answer that we may be able to make to the first of these questions, depends, of course, on our response to the second. It is only out of the experience of communities living as nearly as possible without extrinsic sanctions that we are able to offer a critique of praxis which would validate the claim that Jesus by his life, death and Resurrection has liberated us in a significant way from the tutelage of a law which is necessarily always in some measure alienating and oppressive. What our more usual experience seems to clarify is that any structuring of church or society at large that classifies people so that the decision making is concentrated into the hands of a few, is the entrance into a spiral of intensifying alienation, oppression and violence.

11

Jesus and Marx:

Social Justice and Redemption

It is over this issue of the inner force of the law of freedom in Christ as the transforming power in the human situation, that Christians encounter Marxists.[1] Marxism, while not a religion, is a comprehensive and aggressive doctrine of salvation. Karl Marx, like Jesus of Nazareth, went forth from what might otherwise have been a very comfortable life out of compassion for the bewildered and leaderless masses — out of

---

[1] It should be noted that the Christian-Marxist encounter is not a purely Third World phenomenon but has been prominent and serious in Europe at least since the end of World War II. Many, if not most, of the great European theologians have been involved in it in one way or another.

compassion for their suffering of material want and great burdens of labor, and for their oppression by those who enriched themselves at the expense of poor laboring families, and for their inability to see what caused their alienation from their true human realization.

There is no doubt that the life of Marx, like that of Jesus, was one of self-sacrificing compassionate ministry to others, based on a luminous vision of what human life might be and ought to be and on a burning desire to help bring it about at whatever cost to himself that might entail. Moreover, there is no doubt that, as in the case of Jesus, the compassion of Marx drew him further and further into personal identification with the fate of the poor, for he himself with his family came, by force of circumstances flowing from his devotion to the cause, to live in very wretched conditions.

Marxists, like Christians, are concerned with the redemption of the world, that is of the world of human lives and affairs. What Marxists see as alienation is closely related to what Christians see as the heritage of original sin and pervasive sinfulness.[2] It is closely related because both are concerned with selfishness, greed, injustice and oppression, and with all the consequent suffering inflicted on the powerless. Further, both Marxists and Christians define this condition as an estrangement from what is truly human, and both claim to have a way of redemption from this condition and of reconciliation both for individuals and for society. In the world of

---

[2]*Cf.*, Erich Fromm, *Marx's Concept of Man* (N.Y.: Ungar, 1961); and, among primary sources, Karl Marx, *Basic Writings on Politics and Philosophy*, ed. Lewis Feuer, (N.Y.: Doubleday, 1959); and *Writings of the Young Marx on Philosophy and Society*, translated and edited by Lloyd D. Easton and Kurt Guddat, (N.Y.: Doubleday, 1967).

today it is perhaps with the Marxists most of all that Christians have a very urgent wager with very high stakes.

The Christian reading of sin and redemption centers upon God as the source and meaning and goal of all human existence, and takes Jesus as the revelation of God — Jesus with his Abba-experience of intimacy and compassion. Where life is not centered upon God, there the harmony of human existence and the harmony of human society is broken, compassion is lost and domination and exploitation take its place. To restore the harmony and to aknowledge the dignity of all human persons it is necessary to recapture the orientation of human life to God and to regain the universal compassion that grounds genuine community. Fruitless, needless human suffering is the symptom in which sin and sinfulness manifest themselves, and effective compassion is the sign in which redemptive grace is manifested. That is why the death of Jesus is a redemptive breakthrough of divine power, a breakthrough that we can recognize retrospectively by our own experience of transformation of individuals and societies in the spirit of the Risen Christ.

The Marxist reading of alienation and of the remedial transformation of the quality of human life seems to center on the dialectical process of history in which progressively the dignity of all human persons comes to be honored, particularly their dignity as workers. Marxists, because they do not look beyond human history to a transcendent God, must locate the focus of their hope and their criteria for action appropriate to their hope within the historical process and by reference to the culmination they envisage for that process. They look towards the ideal of a classless society living in a stateless community. Alienation is manifest primarily by the oppression of the worker who is consumed for someone else's profit, and secondarily by the political structure of societies trying to keep the laboring masses in their oppressed condition so as to maintain, enhance and extend the profit-making system at their expense. The sign of liberating breakthroughs that move the historical dialectic toward its culmination is revolution in the structures that keep the laboring classes powerless.

Most Christians seem to take it for granted that the revolution of which Marxists speak and dream is necessarily a violent armed rebellion. This is unfounded. The revolution must be an effective way of getting decision-making power and access to capital resources out of the hands of a few wealthy oppressors (whether these are individuals or multinational corporations) and getting that power into the disposition of the laborers or in the intermediary stages at least into the disposition of those who will effectively represent the interests of the laborers. In principle, such revolutions could be without bloodshed or physical violence of any sort. In practice it is the resistance to sharing power with the laboring classes that decides just how violent the revolutionary action will be.

If violence in itself is not the issue between Christians and Marxists, then some Christians assume it is an intrinsic factor of militant atheism. Historically it is true that Marxism has been dogmatically and militantly atheist and has persecuted active believers doggedly and cruelly in most places where a Communist regime has been established. However, this militant atheism has to be seen in context. The experience that Marx himself and his associate, Engels, had of the functioning of religion in society was such that the role of religion seemed to be to keep the people oppressed and uncritical by giving them a view of the world and their lives within it which located ultimate reality (the really real) outside their experience, their earthly lives and the world's history. Everything that happened and everything they suffered could be viewed as simply the prelude to their proper existence after death, in which justice and happiness would be achieved. This is the source of the famous dictum of Marx and Engels in their *Communist Manifesto* that religion was the opium of the people, that is, that it robbed them of their contact with reality and their interest in it.

Where religion has not been playing this role, Marxist thinkers have become quite ambivalent towards it and have occasionally been willing to collaborate with Christian groups concerned for social justice. However, the habit of opposing religion is so deeply ingrained that most Communist regimes and Marxist thinkers seem to assume that they must do so on principle and that it is the nature of religion to oppress in one way or another.

Nevertheless it is not the persecution of religion which is the basic issue between Marxists and Christians. Nor can it be, as was discussed in the chapter on Buddhism, a case that Marxism looks for worldly redemption and Christianity for spiritual redemption. The real issue seems to be a rather more subtle one concerning the process. It is not the physical violence of armed revolution that is the crux of this but the more subtle violence of manipulation of people into what is judged to be in their own best interests. This is a temptation from which Christians have by no means been immune, though in the Marxist understanding of the process of liberation it is accepted on principle.

Behind this acceptance on principle lies in fact a difference in anthropology which turns out to be significant. In Marxist thought people, for instance, are defined as parts of society and parts of the historical process to such an extent that individual persons can be subordinated to the interests of the process and the present generation can be subordinated to the fulfillment of the dream in the future. This subordination is absolute because there is no expectation of any after-life. Likewise, indoctrination by manipulative means is not contrary to the understanding of the process of liberation because the freedom of the workers and the liberation of the society at large is understood in terms of the relation between work and the worker, not primarily in terms of relationships of love and personal acceptance, and sense of meaning in life. Redemption is expected to work from the outside inwards, from conversion of structures to conversion of individual experience.

Christians have, of course, throughout the ages often been outrageously manipulative at times even to the point of forced mass "conversions" to Christianity. They have done a great deal of bullying and forced reorganizing in the name of Christ. They have even conducted military crusades, though the primary purpose of these was to capture places not people, and they have subdued great populations of the world to colonial domination in the name of Christ, "civilizing" them in the attempt to organize them into the "freedom" of Christian society. Yet, strangely, it is the Communist presence and mode of action in the contemporary world that has confronted Christians with some serious questions about what is really involved in the process of redemption in relation to the social structures of our society.

The Marxist presence in the modern world has been a challenge and a problem for Christians not so much because it offered a worldly redemption that Christians see as reductionist. This could have been pointed out easily enough. But Marxism's real challenge is that it took over a neglected aspect of the Christian (and Jewish) understanding of redemption, namely the concern for what the redemption or liberation of the world from sin means in terms of social justice. This in turn is a matter of the larger structures of society — economic, political and social. It appears to be precisely the neglect of the more radical questions of social justice in the modern world by Christian churches and so-called Christian governments that sparked the reaction that saw the possibility of action for social justice as a strictly atheist option, and one that must be approached by the overthrow, violent if necessary, of most established governments in the world.

The real problem for Christians seems to be that what should have been the Christian concern has been taken over in a name antithetical to the name of Christ and God. A typical Christian reaction to this has been to claim that in the name of Christ we are and always have been concerned for the poor and the oppressed and marginated, but that the way of Jesus is to heal and console and not to stir up revolutions. Some go further and say those very things that caused Marx to identify religion as the opium of the people, exhorting the oppressed and deprived (with whom they have not personally cast in their lot) to suffer patiently and willingly in the name of Jesus expecting their reward for this beyond death. As was pointed out in chapters 5, 6 and 8, this is too passive a reading of the testimonies we have concerning Jesus.

If Jesus is the Word of God spoken to us in history, and if the content of that Word is Compassion, the Compassion of God, indeed the effective Compassion of God redeeming the world from the suffering that is the outcome of the whole heritage of sin, then the Christian answer to the suffering and oppression of our times cannot be as passive as the two answers above indicate. We have means of transforming the knowledge and awareness that people have of the causes of suffering in the economic structures and political organization of the world. We also have ways of influencing the large structures of society, through democratic channels, through organizing popular movements, through rallying world opinion, through strikes and boycotts, through trade embargos and transfer of investments, through lobbying and through the press and media. We have options far beyond anything that Jesus could have dreamed of in his own time and society. The imitation of Christ means the exercise of effective compassion in all the dimensions that are available to us in the circumstances of our time, not in the limited dimensions that were available to him in his time.

Even where this is accepted, there is considerable anxiety among Christians over the fact that in most cases Marxist agents for change have been on the scene before us and have already established some organization and started a groundswell and proposed an economic and political analysis of the causes of oppression. There is a very general fear in the churches that if Christians become involved once the Marxists have made a beginning, the Christians are almost bound to be co-opted into a Marxist project that will carry them into commitments quite contrary to their faith. The only serious comment that can be made about this is that it seems to express very little faith in the power of the Risen Christ operating in his followers to suppose that collaboration for social justice by Christians and Marxists almost surely means a Marxist takeover.

12

Jesus and Gandhi:

Salvation and Non-violence

It is possible that Gandhi understood Jesus better than most Christians will ever do, because he followed his example in those two aspects which seem to have been most central and characteristic of the experience of Jesus and his purpose in life. Those two aspects for both men were intimacy with God and inexhaustible, non-exclusive compassion for people. And those two relationships, with God and with people, were closely connected in the attitude of radical non-violence (named meekness and non-retaliation in the Gospels) and in the attitude of ultimate vulnerability.

Gandhi, like Buddha, Moses, Jesus and Marx, abandoned the comparative comfort of a secure and pleasant life (in his case a promising law practice in South Africa), out of compassion for his oppressed people and the burning desire to liberate them from their oppressors and from their own oppressed consciousness and their failure to act as a people in support of one another's rights. The life of Gandhi offers an imaginative commentary on the life of Jesus, for in Gandhi's case we have his own writings, great detail of his personal spiritual development as well as the progress of his public ministry for the liberation of his people, and carefully researched biographies.[1]

What makes Gandhi particularly interesting in the context of a comparison with Jesus is, that although he expressed deep respect for Jesus and his example, Gandhi was and remained a Hindu (though it seems that he came under the influence of a very ecumenically minded religious leader in his childhood, something that could happen more easily in Hinduism than in most other religious traditions). Moreover, because Gandhi was not always committed to striving after pure non-violence, but came by personal adult reflection to this commitment and conviction, he has left us most careful records of his thinking in the matter.

The life and action of Gandhi is well known and it is not necessary to dwell on it, but his impact on contemporary Christian thought and attitudes and expectations is pertinent to the thesis of this book. The reluctance of Christians to engage in profound social changes for fear of the conflictual

---

[1] *Cf.* Mohandas K. Gandhi, *The Gandhi Sutras*, arranged and introduced by D. S. Sarma (N.Y.: Devin-Adair, 1949); and Mohandas K. Gandhi, *All Men Are Brothers* (N.Y.: Columbia University Press, 1958).

aspects of social and political action for change, as noted in the previous chapter, may be largely due to the fact that they have had no confidence that the way of Jesus would really work as a way of redemption in the world. They have in practice opted for the salvation of souls out of the world and not for the salvation of the world. They have for the most part considered that politics are in a realm apart where religious faith is not competent to scrutinize action. Yet sober reflection will discover that this is idolatrous in the strict sense, inasmuch as it implies that there are realms over which God is not Lord and in which Jesus as the effective Compassion of God can effect no change or conversion.

Christians have feared the conflictual aspects of public life even in a democratic setting and far more in those situations of ruthless dictatorship where liberating, redeeming action could only be by a radical revolution in the structures. In these latter it seems still to be the conviction of most Christians of the Western world that there can be no revolution without armed violence in a military take-over of power which will then have to maintain itself with almost equal violence to prevent a counter-revolution being staged with even greater bloodshed. The dogged insistence that this is inevitable and that therefore the Christian option is to accept the present injustice and oppression as the lesser evil, is grounded in the unquestioned assumption that the way of Jesus does not work. It is the unquestioned assumption that only violence in one form or another can achieve significant change in the world of public affairs.

What the extraordinary life of Gandhi shows is that this is entirely mistaken. Given equal commitment, and a just cause, non-violent action is more effective and is longer lasting in its effects. However, perhaps the more important revelation of Gandhi's ministry is the lack of Christian faith among Christians and the inconsistency between our basic doctrinal positions and our community action in the world. The meekness and non-retaliation of Jesus was not passivity in the situation of oppression in which he found his people. He was most certainly not crucified for staying quietly at home to mind the carpentry business. The preaching and ministry of Jesus was in every way a challenge to the unjust structures of oppression and therefore in every way a provocation to those who profited by them.

This would suggest that the followers of Jesus are not most devout when they quietly avoid involvement in political and public conflictual situations and stay at home "minding their own business." They are most devout and closest to him when they share deeply in his own intimacy with God and therefore find themselves drawn into the divine Compassion in practical and effective ways wherever there is suffering of whatever kind. Where the suffering is the unnecessary burden of unjust structures in society, the Compassion shows itself in an effective challenge.

Perhaps one of the problems is that the culture of the technically oriented and fast changing Western world of our times has crippled our imagination as far as human relations are concerned. As mentioned previously, our predominant image of power is the impersonal one of pushing an object with mechanical force from the outside. We tend to transfer this image to human relations and to think of getting things done by pushing people into doing them. We tend to forget, perhaps, that the basic dynamics of truly effective relationships among people and truly effective community action are invitation and encouragement, compassion and solidarity, truth-speaking in a context of affection and common concern, personal fidelity and risk, listening and challenging consciences, and so forth. We also tend to forget that political action is first and foremost a matter of human relationships, and that Christian political action is a matter of conversion both of hearts and of social structures to the acceptance of God's Reign in human affairs.

It may be because we tend to forget these things that non-violence tends to be a synonym for inactivity among us. The Christian response to political situations of oppression in the West can never be the same after the experience of Gandhi, for he has personified the divine Compassion in our times to an extraordinary degree that echoed the life and ministry of Jesus in unmistakable terms. And indeed the memories which he awoke came to life in Martin Luther King, in Danilo Dolci, in Cesar Chavez, in Oscar Romero, in Helder Camara, in Dorothy Day and in others whose name is legion. This is perhaps the clearest sign that Christ is risen and is among us, for the incarnate Compassion of God is most appropriately and powerfully expressed in non-violent action for justice and peace in the world.

Selected Bibliography

The following is a brief bibliography of books more immediately germane to the thesis of this book. There is no intention to imply that the authors of these titles would approve the thesis of the book. Periodical articles, though cited in the footnotes, have been omitted from the bibliography in the interest of brevity.

New Testament Studies and Portraits of the Historical Jesus

Raymond Brown, *Jesus, God and Man* (Milwaukee: Bruce, 1967)

————————, *The Virginal Conception and Bodily Resurrection of Jesus* (N.Y.: Paulist, 1973)

Richard J. Cassidy, *Jesus, Politics and Society* (Maryknoll: Orbis, 1978)

Oscar Cullmann, *The Christology of the New Testament* (Philadelphia: Westminster, 1963)

————————, *Jesus and the Revolutionaries* (N.Y.: Harper & Row, 1970)

James D.G. Dunn, *Christology in the Making*, (Philadelphia: Westminster, 1980)

David G. Flusser, *Jesus* (N.Y.: Herder, 1969)

Segundo Galilea, *Following Jesus* (Maryknoll: Orbis, 1981)

Ferdinand Hahn, *The Titles of Jesus in Christology* (N.Y.: World Publishing, 1969)

Martin Hengel, *Was Jesus a Revolutionist?* (Philadelphia: Fortress, 1971)

Martin Hengel, *Son of God* (Philadelphia: Fortress, 1976)

Joachim Jeremias, *The Parables of Jesus* (N.Y.: Scribner, 1963)

──────────, *The Eucharistic Words of Jesus* (N.Y.: Scribner, 1966)

──────────, *New Testament Theology*. Vol.I. (N.Y.: Scribner, 1971)

Ernest Käsemann, *Jesus Means Freedom* (Philadelphia: Fortress, 1972

Willi Marxsen, *The Resurrection of Jesus of Nazareth* (Philadelphia: Fortress, 1972)

Albert Nolan, *Jesus before Christianity* (Maryknoll: Orbis, 1978)

Rudolf Schnackenburg, *God's Rule and Kingdom* (N.Y.: Herder, 1963

Gerard Sloyan, *Jesus on Trial* (Philadelphia: Fortress, 1973)

John Howard Yoder, *The Politics of Jesus* (Grand Rapids: Eerdmans, 1972)

History of Christology

Aloys Grillmeier, *Christ in Christian Tradition* (Atlanta: John Knox, 1975)

J.N.D. Kelly, *Early Christian Doctrines* (N.Y.: Harper, 1978)

Bernard Lonergan, *The Way to Nicea* (Philadelphia: Wesminster, 1976)

Richard A. Norris, *The Christological Controversy* (Philadelphia: Fortress, 1980)

Systematic Christology

Leonardo Boff, *Christ the Liberator* (Maryknoll: Orbis, 1978)

Michael L. Cook, *The Jesus of Faith* (N.Y.: Paulist, 1981)

Hans Frei, *The Identity of Jesus* (Philadelphia: Fortress, 1973)

Peter Hodgson, *Jesus: Word and Presence* (Philadelphia: Fortress, 1971)

Walter Kaspar, *Jesus, the Christ* (N.Y.: Paulist, 1977)

Kazoh Kitamori, *The Theology of the Pain of God* (Richmond: John Knox, 1967)

Hans Küng, *On Being a Christian* (N.Y.: Doubleday, 1976)

Jurgen Moltmann, *The Crucified God* (N.Y.: Harper, 1974)

Wolfhart Pannenberg, *Jesus, God and Man* (Philadelphia: Westminster, 1968)

John T. Pawlikowski, *Christ in the Light of the Christian-Jewish Dialogue* (N.Y.: Paulist, 1982)

Edward Schillebeeckx, *Christ, The Sacrament of the Encounter with God* (N.Y.: Sheed & Ward, 1963)

——————————, *Jesus: An Experiment in Christology* (N.Y.: Seabury, 1979)

——————————, *Christ: The Experience of Jesus as Lord* (N.Y.: Seabury, 1980)

——————————, *Interim Report on the Books, Jesus and Christ* (N.Y.: Crossroad, 1982)

Piet Schoonenberg, *The Christ* (N.Y.: Herder, 1971)

Jon Sobrino, *Christology at the Crossroads* (Maryknoll: Orbis, 1978)

George H. Tavard, *Images of the Christ* (Washington: University of America Press, 1982)

Frans Jozef van Beeck, *Christ Proclaimed: Christology as Rhetoric* (N.Y.: Paulist, 1979)

Symposia

Thomas E. Clarke, ed., *Above Every Name: The Lordship of Christ and Social Systems* (N.Y.: Paulist, 1980)

Edward Schillebeeckx and Bonifaas Willems, eds., *Who is Jesus of Nazareth?* (N.Y.: Paulist, 1966)

Edward Schillebeeckx and Bas van Iersel, eds., *Jesus Christ and Human Freedom* (N.Y.: Herder, 1974)

Edward Schillebeeckx and J.B. Metz, eds., *Jesus, Son of God?* (N.Y.: Seabury, 1982)

S.W. Sykes and J.P. Clayton, eds., *Christ, Faith and History.* (N.Y.: Cambridge University Press, 1972).